KU-464-051

North Staffordshire Press

PIT BOY TO PRIME MINISTER

Loosely based on the book 'Pit Boy to Prime Minister' by G. Bebbington

Edward Hilton

Pit Boy To Prime Minister

All Rights Reserved

© *Copyright Edward Hilton*

No part of this book may be reproduced in any form by photocopying or any electronic or mechanical means, including information storage and retrieval systems, without permission in writing from both the copyright owner and the publisher of this book.

ISBN 978-1-9160152-2-7

Published in 2019

North Staffordshire Press

10 Queen Street

Newcastle-under-Lyme

ST5 1ED

ACKNOWLEDGEMENTS

Firstly, I would like to thank all of my family and friends, without whom none of this would be possible.

In particular, I would like to thank:

Helen and Bill Hilton

Jane Young

Jack and Gemma Tomson

Lesley and Gary Coe

Marcus Taylor

Jane and Martin Fry

Alan Hilton and Denise Rigby

A number of anonymous sponsors

I would also like to thank Malcolm Henson and the team at North Staffordshire Press, Graham Bebbington for his permission to adapt this play from his book and The Engelsea Brook Methodist Museum for background information about Methodism in Stoke on Trent.

Finally, I would like to thank Karen Fenton for her advice in editing and preparing the play for the stage.

CHARACTERS

JOSEPH COOK	Public Speaker for Free Trade and Politician
MARY TURNER	Joseph's future wife
ARTHUR HASSAM	Joseph's lifelong friend
SIR WILLIAM LYNE	Former friend of Joseph and Rival Protectionist Politician
ANDREW FISHER	Labour Politician
ALFRED DEAKIN	Protectionist Politician
JOHN SHENTON	Chapel Official/Bible Teacher
WILLIAM M. HUGHES	Labour Politician and Ally of Joseph Cook
MARGARET COOKE	Joseph's mother
FRANCIS STANIER	Mayor of Silverdale
GEORGE COOK	Joseph and Mary's eldest son
KING GEORGE V	King of England
MINER	Miner at the Silverdale Collieries
EDMUND BARTON	Protectionist Politician
GEORGE REID	Free Trader Politician

EXTRAS

MINE WORKERS

JOSEPH'S SIBLINGS

JOSEPH AND MARY'S CHILDREN

POLITICIANS AND OFFICIALS

PEOPLE

"Though Black I am and hidden away
For millions and millions of years,
I have my price and some must pay
In sweat and blood and tears…

O God of mercy, will it ever be
That safety for the miner we shall see?
Will he be wholly free from dread,
Whilst down the mine to earn his
bread?"

J. Rusby

JOSEPH COOK'S REMARKABLE LIFE STORY
BEGINS IN THE WORKING-CLASS COMMUNITY OF
SILVERDALE, STOKE ON TRENT. THE USE OF
LOCAL DIALECT IN THE SCRIPT ILLUSTRATES
HIS DEVELOPMENT FROM A LOWLY MINER TO A
WELL-EDUCATED POLITICIAN.

ACT I

SCENE 1

(SILVERDALE, 1873. THE COOKE HOUSEHOLD. MARGARET COOKE AND CHILDREN ARE ONSTAGE TO ONE SIDE PLAYING.

ENTER COOK AND MINER SILENTLY TOGETHER FROM THE OTHER SIDE OF THE STAGE.)

<u>MINER</u>

MRS COOKE MET I SPAKE WITH YOR A MOMENT?

<u>MARGARET COOKE</u>

AYE, OF COURSE YOU CAN. COME IN.

(COOK CONTINUES TO CRY)

WHAT'S DOIN'? IS JOSEPH OW RATE?

<u>MINER</u>

(REMOVES CAP)

YOU MUST KNOWST, THIS IS SUMMAT THAT AFFECTS YOURSEN AND THE YOUNG 'UNS. I BELIEVE IT BEST THAT YOUNG MASTER COOK BE THE ONE TO TELL YER.

(TO COOK)

GO AHEAD KIDDA.

<u>COOK</u>

(THROUGH TEARS AND SNIFFLES)

AR DUNNA KNOWST IF AR CAN.

1

MINER

YOU 'AVE NOWT TER MITHER ABOUT MASTER COOK. JUST TAKE YER TIME
AN'.

MARGARET COOKE

WHAT'S DOIN' JOSEPH?

COOK

(*THROUGH TEARS AND SNIFFLES*)

FAETHER AND AR WERE WORKING DOWN IN TH' PIT AND…

(*BURSTS INTO TEARS*)

MINER

AR AM REET SORRY MRS COOKE, BUT THERE WUZ A MININ' ACCIDENT
TODAY. AND IT IS ME DUTY TER TELL YER THAT YOWER 'USBAND IS
JED.

MARGARET COOKE

(*DISTRAUGHTLY*)

'OW 'AS THIS 'APPENED? PLEASE TELL ME EVERYTHIN' YER KEN.

MINER

JOSEPH WAS WORKIN' WITH WILLIAM, OO WAS MENDIN' THE RAILS IN
TH' MINE WHEN TH' BRAKES OF TH' WAGON GAVE OUT. JOSEPH DIDNA
KNOWST WHAT WAS 'APPENIN', BUT YOWER 'USBAND SAW TH' DANGER
AND PUSHED TH' YOUNG LAD OUT THE WAY BEFORE THE WAGON COULD
'ARM 'IM. AR AM AFRAID WILLIAM WAS 'IMSELF KILLED.

(*PAUSE*)

DUST WISH ME TER CONTINUE?

2

MARGARET COOKE

AR DUNNA KNOWST. I MITHER FOR THE CHILDREN, BUT MOST OF ALL
JOSEPH. 'IS FAETHER WUZ TH' APPLE OF 'IS EYE. NOW WILLIAM IS
GONE AR DUNNA KNOWST WHAT ME SON IS GOIN' TER DO. THANK YER
FOR BRINGIN' 'IM BACK TER ME.

MINER

(*AWKWARD TONE*)

I'LL LEAVE YER BE THEN. BUT IF YER NEED SOMEONE TER TALK TER
YOU CAN TALK TER TH' PRIMITIVE METHODISTS. THEY 'AVE 'ELPED ME
MATES AND AR VERY WELL OVER TH' YEARS.

MARGARET COOKE

THANK YER, THANK YER VERY MUCH.

(*EXIT MINER*)

MARGARET COOKE

JOSEPH, 'OW ARE YER FEELING?

COOK

PLEASE, JUST LEAVE ME BE MOTHER.

MARGARET COOKE

AR AM SO SORRY ABOUT WHAT 'AVEN 'APPENED, BUT YER NOW TH' MAN
OF TH' 'OUSE. WITH YOWER FAETHER GONE WE MUST ALL RELY ON WHAT
LITTLE PITTANCE YER CAN EARN FROM TH' MINES.

COOK

MOTHER, PLEASE. PLEASE DUNNA SEND ME BACK DOWN TER THAT HELL!
IT BE TH' LAST PLACE AR WISH TER RETURN TER!

3

MARGARET COOKE

BUT WITHOUT A STEADY INCOME WE WUNNA BE ABLE TER MANAGE AS A
FAMILY. WE NEED MONEY NOW MORE THAN EVER. THIS IS SUMMAT YER
MUST DO.

COOK

AR DUNNA KNOWST ABOUT THIS.

MARGARET COOKE

AR KNOW LOSING YOWER FAETHER IS 'ARD, BUT WE 'AVE ALREADY 'AD
TER STOP YER SCHOOLIN' BECAUSE OF OUR MONEY PROBLEMS. WITH
ANOTHER BABY ON TH' WAY, WITHOUT A BREADWINNER OUR FAMILY
COULD BE IN REET TROUBLE.

COOK

WELL IF AR MUST DO THIS FOR TH' GOOD OF OURSEN, THEN THAT IS
WHAT AR SHALL DO.

MARGARET COOKE

YER A GOOD KIDDA JOSEPH. IF YER NEED ME 'ELP WITH ANYTHIN',
YOU 'AVE BUT TER ASK. BUT MEBBE WE SHOULD LOOK TER TH'
PRIMITIVE METHODISTS TER 'ELP US.

(EXEUNT)

ACT I

SCENE 2

(THE PRIMITIVE METHODIST CHAPEL. SHENTON IS PREACHING TO THE VILLAGERS INCLUDING ARTHUR.)

SHENTON

MY GOOD FRIENDS, I SAY TO YOU NOW THAT YOU MUST NOT TAKE THE THINGS YOU ARE GIVEN, FOR FREE, EVERYDAY, FOR GRANTED.

(ENTER MARGARET COOKE AND JOSEPH)

MARGARET COOKE

IS EVERYTHING OW RATE JOSEPH?

COOK

AR AM FINE. YER DUNNA NEED TER BE SO CONCERNED FOR ME MA, AR AM NOT A KIDDA ANYMORE. AR CAN TAKE CARE A MESEN.

MARGARET COOKE

JOSEPH! YER NEDNA BE LIKE THIS. WE CAME TER ATTEND TH' SERVICE NOT TER GAUP ABOUT WHAT 'APPENED.

COOK

AR AM SORRY. AR NEED SOME TIME FO' MESEN TER THINK ABOUT TH' FUTURE. FORGIVE ME IF I CHOOSE TER SIT ALONE.

(COOK MOVES AWAY AND SITS SOMEWHERE ELSE)

MARGARET COOKE

BE CAREFUL.

SHENTON

(TO CROWD)

JESUS ONCE TAUGHT US TO CHERISH THE THINGS THAT WE ARE GIVEN IN LIFE, AND I BELIEVE THIS IS SHOWN GREATLY IN MY TEXT FOR TODAY: CORINTHIANS 6:19-20. WOULD ANYONE CARE TO READ THE PASSAGE?

(ARTHUR STANDS UP)

ARTHUR

AR WILL.

SHENTON

COME UP THEN MY BROTHER, AND READ FROM THE HOLY TEXT.

ARTHUR

DID YOU NOT KNOW THAT YOUR BODIES ARE TEMPLES OF THE 'OLY SPIRIT, OO IS IN YOU, OOM YOU 'AVE RECEIVED FROM GOD? YOU ARE NOT YOUR OWN; YOU WERE BOUGHT AT A PRICE. THEREFORE, 'ONOUR GOD WITH YOUR BODIES.

SHENTON

THANK YOU BROTHER ARTHUR FOR THAT BRILLIANT READING. IT WAS VERY GOOD INDEED AND WE CAN LEARN A LOT FROM THE MESSAGE IT PRESENTS. BY CHERISHING THOSE THINGS THAT GOD GAVE TO YOU, IN RETURN YOU OFFER YOURSELF TO THE LORD. LOVE AND GOD GO HAND IN HAND TOGETHER, AND I BELIEVE THAT AT THE HEART OF THIS RELATIONSHIP IS THE FAMILY. AFTER ALL, WHAT CREATES MORE LOVE THAN THE FAMILY?

(ARTHUR SITS DOWN NEXT TO JOSEPH)

COOK

AR THOUGHT YER READ THAT VERY WELL. RELIGION IS NOT SUMMAT AR 'AVE FOUND VERY INTERESTIN', BUT THAT LESSON REALLY SPOKE TER ME.

ARTHUR

THANK YER VERY MUCH. I DUNNA BELIEVE WE 'AVE MET BEFORE.

COOK

OH. JOSEPH COOK.

(*OFFERS HAND TO ARTHUR*)

ARTHUR

ARTHUR 'ASSAM, FEELING VERY PLEASED TER MEET YER JOSEPH COOK.

COOK

PLEASED TER MAKE YOWER ACQUAINTANCE.

ARTHUR

YER KNOWST, YER ARE NOT ALONE IN YOWER LOSS.

COOK

'OW CAN YER TELL I'VE LOST SOMEONE?

ARTHUR

AR KEN BECAUSE AR TOO 'AVE LOST ME FAETHER TER TH' MINES, AND AR WUZ AS YER ARE RIGHT NOW. AR WANT TER TELL YER THAT YER HAVE NOWT TER FEAR. IT MAY BE PAININ' YER NOW, BUT YER 'AVE YOWER WHOLE LIFE IN FRONT OF YER.

COOK

AR DIDNA THINK OF IT LIKE THAT. AR MUST GET ON WITH ME LIFE, AND THERE IS NO POINT BATHERING ON ABOUT 'ARD TIMES. YER 'AVE DEALT WITH YOURS, SO THERE INNA A REASON AR CANNA DO THE SAME. THANK YOU ARTHUR.

ARTHUR

AR 'AVE BEEN ABLE TO COPE WELL SINCE ME FAETHER DIED. BUT WHAT REALLY 'ELPED ME THROUGH ME STRUGGLE WERE THE PRAYER MEETINGS 'OSTED BY MR SHENTON.

COOK

PRAYER MEETINGS? AR DUNNA KNOWST IF AR WOULD FIND THOSE INTERESTIN'.

ARTHUR

(*CHUCKLES*)

MR SHENTON TAUGHT ME MORE THAN JUST WHAT TH' BIBLE PREACHES. 'E TAUGHT ME 'OW TER COPE WITH ME LOSS, TER THINK ABOUT ME ACTIONS. AND MOST IMPORTANTLY TER LEARN TER LIVE AND ENJOY ME LIFE AGAIN.

COOK

AR AM STILL NOT SURE. GOD 'AS NOT SHOWN ME THAT 'E 'AS TH' ANSWERS FOR A LIFE LIKE MINE.

ARTHUR

AR USED TER THINK THAT WAY AS WELL, BUT AR NOW FEEL THAT TH' LESSONS OF TH' BIBLE ARE MORE IMPORTANT BECAUSE OF TH' MORALS THEY TEACH US.

(*SHENTON JOINS COOK AND ARTHUR*)

SHENTON

YOU ARE VERY RIGHT BROTHER ARTHUR. IF YOU JUST FOCUS ON THE MESSAGE THAT THE BIBLE TEACHES, THEN EVERYTHING MAKES A LOT MORE SENSE. I SEE YOU'VE MADE A NEW FRIEND.

ARTHUR

AYE.

(*TO COOK*)

JOSEPH, THIS IS MR SHENTON, ACTIN' REVEREND OF TH' SILVERDALE PRIMITIVE METHODISTS SINCE REVEREND GRIFFIN LEFT A FEW MONTHS AGO.

SHENTON

WELCOME TO OUR HOME JOSEPH. I HOPE YOU FEEL AT PEACE HERE.

ARTHUR

JOSEPH IS IN TH' SAME PLACE AS AR WUZ AFTER AR 'AD LOST ME FAETHER. AR TOLD 'IM ABOUT YOWER WEEKLY PRAYER MEETIN'S.

SHENTON

OH, ARE YOU INTERESTED IN JOINING, JOSEPH?

COOK

ARTHUR TELLS ME THAT YER 'AVE BEEN ABLE TER 'ELP 'IM THROUGH 'IS STRUGGLES, AND AR AM NOW GOIN' THROUGH TH' SAME THING. TH' MINES ARE A WORLD OF BRUTAL LABOUR AND IT SUCKS TH' ENERGY FROM ME BONES EVERY DAY. MY FAMILY NEEDS ME TO PROVIDE FOR THEM NOW AND AR WAS WONDERIN' IF YER 'ELP ME LIKE YER 'AVE DONE WITH ARTHUR?

SHENTON

WELL, OUR WEEKLY MEETINGS USUALLY CONSIST OF PRAYER READINGS AND DISCUSSION, BUT WE CAN TURN OUR MINDS TO ANY PROBLEM THAT MAY BE TROUBLING YOU.

COOK

THANK YER! THANK YER SO MUCH! AR SHALL ATTEND!

SHENTON

SPLENDID! OUR CIRCLE USUALLY MEETS EVERY SATURDAY AFTERNOON AT MY HOUSE.

COOK

AR SHALL SEE YER AT TH' NIGHEST MEETIN' THEN.

ARTHUR

WE SHALL SEE YER THERE, JOSEPH!

(EXIT SHENTON AND ARTHUR)

MARGARET COOKE

AY UP JOSEPH, WE MUST BE OFF WOM SOON. AR SAW YER TALKIN' TER TH' REVEREND. WHAT WERE YER TALKIN' ABOUT?

COOK

ARTHUR AND AR WERE TALKIN' ABOUT TH' REVEREND'S REGULAR PRAYER MEETIN'S.

MARGARET COOKE

OH AYE? ARE YER INTERESTED IN GOIN'?

COOK

AYE. THEY APPEAR TER 'AVE 'ELPED ARTHUR VERY WELL, SO AR WOULD LIKE TER GO AND SEE IF THESE MEETIN'S CAN 'ELP ME AN ALL.

MARGARET COOKE

AR THANK TH' LORD FOR YOWER SUPPORT. IN TIME YER WILL DO GREAT THINGS, AR KNOWST IT.

(EXEUNT)

ACT I

SCENE 3

(SHENTON'S HOUSE. SHENTON'S PRAYER MEETING IS IN SESSION WITH JOSEPH, ARTHUR AND MARY IN ATTENDANCE.)

SHENTON

I WOULD LIKE TO THANK ALL OF YOU FOR BEING ABLE TO MAKE IT TO THE MEETING TODAY. WE HAVE A NEW MEMBER JOINING OUR CIRCLE AND I THINK WE WOULD APPRECIATE IT IF HE COULD INTRODUCE HIMSELF TO US.

COOK

AR AM NOT SO GOOD AT INTRODUCTIONS MR SHENTON.

SHENTON

PLEASE, DO NOT BE SHY MY BROTHER. YOU ARE MOST WELCOME TO INTRODUCE YOURSELF AS YOU SEE FIT. WE ARE ALL EAGER TO LEARN ABOUT THE YOUNG MAN WHO HAS COME BEFORE US TODAY.

(COOK STANDS UP)

COOK

VERY WELL. ME NAME IS JOSEPH COOK AND AR 'AVE RECENTLY JOINED THE PRIMITIVE METHODISTS. AR LOST ME FATHER TER THE MINES, AND SINCE THEN AR 'AVE BEEN STRUGGLIN' TO FIND A PATH FORWARD FROM WHAT 'APPENED.

SHENTON

MAY THE LORD BLESS YOUR COURAGE. AND WHAT IS IT YOU SEEK NOW?

COOK

AR REMEMBER WHAT ME FAETHER TOLD ME BEFORE 'E DIED. 'E TOLD ME TER ALWAYS VALUE ME FAMILY. SO AR WILL. AR 'AVE MADE A PROMISE TER BE THERE FOR THEM, FOR AS LONG AS THEY NEED ME.

11

SHENTON

WELL JOSEPH; THOUGH WE CANNOT BRING YOUR FATHER BACK, WE CAN HELP YOU HONOUR YOUR PROMISE IN MEMORY OF HIM.

COOK

THANK YER MR SHENTON.

(COOK SITS DOWN)

SHENTON

NOW, TO BUSINESS. JOSEPH, DO YOU KNOW WHAT WE DO AT THESE MEETINGS?

COOK

AR THINK SO. ARTHUR SAID THAT WE TALK ABOUT TH' LESSONS OF GOD, AND THEIR EFFECTS ON TH' COMMUNITY.

SHENTON

THAT IS CORRECT. BUT ARE YOU FAMILIAR WITH THE APPROPRIATE CUSTOMS TO DO SO?

COOK

AR AM AFRAID THESE CUSTOMS 'ANNA BEEN TOLD TER ME.

SHENTON

IN THAT CASE, WE CAN SHOW YOU NOW. ARTHUR, CAN YOU READY A BREW?

ARTHUR

AYE.

(EXIT ARTHUR)

COOK

SO, WHAT EXACTLY ARE THESE CUSTOMS?

MARY

IF I MAY ANSWER YOUR QUESTION BROTHER COOK. WE MEET AND DRINK TEA, WHILE TALKING ABOUT THE WAYS GOD HAS TOUCHED OUR LIVES. YOUR TIE IS SLIGHTLY UNDONE BY THE WAY.

COOK

OH, THANK YER. SORRY, 'AVE WE MET?

SHENTON

BROTHER COOK, THIS IS ONE OUR BRIGHTEST AND HARDEST WORKING COLLEAGUES: SISTER MARY TURNER. SHE HAS COME ALL THE WAY FROM CHESTERTON TO BE HERE TODAY.

COOK

PLEASED TER MEET YER SISTER MARY AND, THANK YER FOR POINTIN' OUT TH' TIE.

(COOK FUMBLES WITH HIS TIE. HE AND MARY SMILE AT EACH OTHER.)

SHENTON

I MUST SAY, NOW I LOOK CLOSER AT YOUR TIE IT IS QUITE INTRIGUING, BROTHER JOSEPH. NOW WHEN BROTHER ARTHUR RETURNS WITH THE TEA WE CAN BEGIN THE DISCUSSIONS.

(ENTER ARTHUR WITH LOVING CUP)

SHENTON

WOULD YOU LIKE TO DEMONSTRATE HOW WE HOLD OUR MEETINGS SISTER MARY?

MARY

I THINK THAT IS AN EXCELLENT IDEA MR SHENTON.

(THE CUP IS PASSED TO MARY)

THIS WEEK HAS BEEN VERY SPECIAL, AS I HAVE HAD THE CHANCE TO
HELP SO MANY PEOPLE. THERE ARE NO DOUBTS IN MY MIND THAT THIS
IS THE WORK OF THE LORD, AND I FEEL VERY PRIVILEGED TO ENACT
THE LOVE OF GOD UPON THE PEOPLE OF THIS VILLAGE.

(MARY DRINKS FROM THE CUP)

SHENTON

THAT IS VERY IMPRESSIVE SISTER MARY. DO YOU FEEL AS IF THESE
EXPERIENCES HAVE HELPED YOU TO GROW AS A PERSON?

MARY

I DO. IT IS A TRULY WONDERFUL FEELING TO HAVE, KNOWING THAT
YOU ARE HELPING OTHER PEOPLE, THAT YOU ARE HELPING THEM TO
INCREASE THEIR KNOWLEDGE ABOUT THE WORLD. BUT IT STILL IS NOT
THE MOST SATISFYING FEELING I HAVE HAD THIS WEEK.

COOK

CAN YER SHARE THAT WITH US TOO?

MARY

I CAN. I HAVE BEEN HELPING INJURED WORKERS FROM THE
COLLIERIES. I FEEL THAT THE PEOPLE WHO WORK IN THE MINES
DESERVE OUR HELP.

COOK

THAT IS VERY SELFLESS OF YER SISTER MARY. MAY AR ASK WHY YER
GO OUT OF YOWER WAY TER 'ELP PEOPLE LIKE THIS?

MARY

I BELIEVE THAT THIS IS WHAT GOD WISHES ME TO DO. I FEEL THAT YOU NEED TO BE RESPONSIBLE WHEN YOU HAVE PEOPLE IN YOUR CARE, AND THE MINERS ARE PEOPLE WHO NEED MY HELP. THIS IS MY WAY OF BRINGING HIS WORK TO THE PEOPLE.

ARTHUR

NOT ONLY THAT, BUT YER APPEAR TER BE SHEPHERDIN' A FLOCK LIKE A LOVIN' GOD WOULD.

SHENTON

EXACTLY ARTHUR! EXACTLY! WOULD YOU LIKE TO GO NEXT?

(MARY PASSES CUP TO ARTHUR)

ARTHUR

AR SHALL. AR CANNA RECALL MANY INSTANCES WHERE GOD 'AS IMPACTED ON ME LIFE THIS WEEK, BEING THAT AR SPENT MOEST OF IT DOWN TH' MINES.

SHENTON

SURELY GOD MUST HAVE TOUCHED YOUR LIFE IN SOME WAY THIS PAST WEEK MY BROTHER.

ARTHUR

AR DO FEEL THAT TH' CLOSEST AR 'AVE COME TER GODLINESS THIS WEEK IS MAKIN' A NEW FRIEND WITH BROTHER COOK 'ERE.

COOK

THANK YER ARTHUR.

ARTHUR

NO AR MEAN IT. IF YER THINK ABOUT IT, OUR SITUATION WAS TH'
SAME AS MARY'S. AR WANTED TO 'ELP YOU BY INTRODUCIN' YER TER
OUR CIRCLE 'ERE. AR WANT TER BE THERE FOR YER, BROTHER.

(COOK STANDS UP)

COOK

THANK YER ALL SO MUCH. ALL OF YER. YER 'AVE MADE ME FEEL VERY
WELCOME 'ERE. AR AM 'UMBLED AND LOST FOR WORDS.

SHENTON

WELL BROTHER JOSEPH, WE ARE GLAD WE ARE HERE TO HELP. WHEN
ARTHUR CAME TO US HE WAS ALMOST AS DISTRAUGHT AS YOU. AND JUST
BY SHARING YOUR PROBLEMS WITH US WE CAN HELP YOU OVERCOME
THEM. UNFORTUNATELY, WE NOW HAVE TO DRAW OUR MEETING TO A
CLOSE BECAUSE WE HAVE RUN OUT OF TIME. UNLESS THERE IS
ANYTHING ELSE ANYONE WOULD LIKE TO SHARE?

COOK

NO.

(ARTHUR SHAKES HIS HEAD)

MARY

NO THANK YOU.

SHENTON

IF THAT IS EVERYTHING, I SHALL SEE YOU TOMORROW THEN.

(EXIT SHENTON)

ARTHUR

JOSEPH, AR SHALL SEE YER NIGHEST AND THEN AT TH' MINE AYE?

                              COOK

                 INDEED, BROTHER. SEE YER THEN.

                        (EXIT ARTHUR)

                              MARY

               JOSEPH, DO YOU HAVE A MINUTE?

                              COOK

                           YES MARY?

                              MARY

     DO YOU THINK IT IS A GOOD IDEA TO BE GOING DOWN THE MINES
          STRAIGHT AFTER YOU LOST YOUR FATHER TO THEM?

                              COOK

     AR AGREE WITH YER. AR DUNNA LIKE TH' WORLD OF TH' MINES, YET
            AR ENDURE THEM, FOR THE SAKE OF ME FAMILY.

                              MARY

      I FEEL VERY UNCOMFORTABLE ABOUT THIS. I HAVE SEEN THE
              SILVERDALE COLLIERIES CLAIM MANY LIVES.

                              COOK

     AR KNOWST. BUT AS YER SAID, WE MUST BE RESPONSIBLE FOR TH'
     PEOPLE WE TAKE CARE OF. AR NEED TER TAKE CARE OF ME FAMILY AND
     TH' ONLY WAY TER DO SO IS BY WORKIN' IN TH' MINE. AR 'AVE
             NOTHIN' ELSE AS ME EDUCATION HAS STOPPED.

                              MARY

     PERHAPS I CAN HELP YOU WITH THAT. I DO HAVE A PASSION FOR
     TEACHING AND YOU HAVE A DESIRE TO LEARN. WE SHARE A LOVE OF
            KNOWLEDGE AND A CURIOSITY ABOUT THE WORLD.

                               17

COOK

AR MUST SAY, IT WOULD BE NICE TO LEARN ABOUT NEW THINGS. WORKIN' AT THE MINE IS VERY BORIN'.

MARY

I CAN IMAGINE. TOILING AT THE COALFACE FOR DAYS, WORKING SEEMINGLY WITHOUT END.

COOK

AR THINK YER OVER EXAGGERATIN' WHAT'S DOIN' SISTER MARY.

MARY

MAYBE. I DO HEAR A LOT OF STORIES FROM THE MINERS. BUT I WISH TO HELP YOU RECOVER, AND I RECKON A LITTLE TUTORING WILL BE PERFECT.

COOK

AYE, THAT SOUNDS VERY GOOD TER ME.

MARY

IT DOES.

COOK

MAYBE WE CAN GO FOR A WALK IN TH' COUNTRYSIDE. TOGETHER.

MARY

I WOULD LIKE THAT JOSEPH. I WOULD LIKE THAT VERY MUCH.

(EXEUNT TOGETHER)

ACT I

SCENE 4

(A SINGLE SPOTLIGHT ON JOSEPH AND ARTHUR. THEY ARE WORKING AT THE MINES. JOSEPH TAKES SURREPTITIOUS LOOKS AT A PAMPHLET.)

(IN WHISPERED TONES)

ARTHUR

JOSEPH, DO YER 'AVE A MOMENT?

COOK

CAN IT WAIT A SECOND?

ARTHUR

'ANG ON. ARE YER READIN' DURIN' SHIFT?

COOK

SHHH! KEEP QUIET!

ARTHUR

JOSEPH, IF TH' BUTTY MAN CATCHES YER READING ON SHIFT 'E WILL 'AVE YOWER GUTS FOR GARTERS.

COOK

EXACTLY. THAT IS WHY AR AM TRYIN' TER KEEP IT QUIET.

ARTHUR

WHAT ARE YER READIN' JOSEPH?

COOK

EVER 'EARD OF TRADE UNIONS ARTHUR?

ARTHUR

TH' NAME SOUNDS FAMILIAR, BUT I CANNA RECALL ANY INFORMATION
ABOUT TH' SUBJECT. REFRESH ME MEMORY.

COOK

SISTER MARY 'AS RECENTLY BEEN TUTORIN' ME ON TH' SUBJECT. AR
FIND IT TO BE VERY INTERESTIN'.

ARTHUR

VERY NICE JOSEPH, BUT WHAT IS YOWER POINT?

COOK

ME POINT IS, TRADE UNIONS 'AVE A LOT TO DO WITH WHAT GOES ON
AT TH' MINES. AR BELIEVE THAT TH' RIGHTS OF THE WORKER SHOULD
BE VALUED JUST AS MUCH AS THAT OF TH' ESTABLISHMENT.

ARTHUR

EVERY MAN SHOULD BE ENTITLED TO 'IS WORK. AROUND HERE,
EVERYONE EXPECTS TO WORK DOWN TH' MINES, IT IS A PART OF OUR
CULTURE.

COOK

REET, AND FROM WHAT AR 'AVE READ ON TRADE UNIONS ME BEST GUESS
IS THE REASON THE ESTABLISHMENT 'AS TRIED TER STOP SUCH UNIONS
IN TH' PAST, IS BECAUSE THEY 'AVE BEEN SCARED OF TH' CHANGES
THEY WOULD DEMAND.

ARTHUR

CHANGE CAN BE A DIFFICULT THING TER 'ANDLE.

COOK

AR GUESS SO, BUT AR STILL BELIEVE IN TH' IDEA OF A WORKPLACE MERITOCRACY.

ARTHUR

SLOW DOWN KIDDA. CAN YER EXPLAIN WHAT A MERITOCRACY IS TER ME? AR 'AVE NO IDEA WHAT YER TALKING ABOUT.

COOK

IT IS SIMPLE ENOUGH TER KNOWST. A MERITOCRACY IS A SOCIETY IN WHICH THE 'ARD WORKING PERSEVERE AND TH' LAZY BECOME… LESS WELL OFF.

ARTHUR

'OW DO YER KNOWST ALL THESE THINGS JOSEPH?

COOK

THAT IS WHY AR READ. AR READ TO EDUCATE MESEN, TO GAIN A GREATER KNOWLEDGE AND UNDERSTANDIN' OF THE THINGS THAT MATTER IN LIFE. MARY 'ELPS ME TER DO THIS, AND AR APPRECIATE EVERYTHIN' SHE DOES FOR ME. BUT AR REMEMBER WHAT ME FAETHER ALWAYS SAID TO ME, HE SAID "JOSEPH ME LAD, WORK IS THE RENT ONE MUST PAY FOR LIFE". JUST THAT PHRASE OVER AND OVER AGAIN.

ARTHUR

DID YER EVER UNDERSTAND WHAT 'E MEANT BY IT?

COOK

AR DINNA AT THE TIME. AR ALWAYS THOUGHT IT WAS SOMETHIN' TO DO WITH TH' WAGES 'E RECEIVED, BUT AR 'AVE ONLY RECENTLY BEGUN TER UNDERSTAND IT.

ARTHUR

SHHHHH, KEEP QUIET. TH' BUTTY MAN IS 'ERE.

(THE BUTTY MAN WALKS PAST COOK AND ARTHUR AS THEY CONTINUE TO WORK HARD.)

COOK

IT MEANS THAT IF YER WORK 'ARD AND PUT TH' EFFORT INTO WHAT YER DO, YER WILL BE UNDOUBTEDLY SUCCESSFUL.

ARTHUR

YOWER FAETHER WAS A VERY WISE MAN JOSEPH. AND A CREDIT TO EVERYONE AT TH' COLLIERIES.

COOK

'E WAS A GOOD BUTTY MAN TER US ALL.

ARTHUR

AYE, 'E WAS. YER KNOW; IF YER THINK ABOUT IT, THERE IS SOME TRUTH IN WHAT YOWER FATHER SAID ABOUT WAGES. IF YER WORK 'ARD YER EARN YOWER WAGES, BUT IF YER WORK 'ARDER THAN EVERYONE ELSE YER COULD GET A BONUS.

COOK

UNDER ME FAETHER MAYBE, BUT THIS NEW BUTTY MAN? IMPOSSIBLE. MARY AND AR FEEL VERY STRONGLY THAT EVEN THOUGH 'E IS OUR EMPLOYER 'E IS BEIN' UNUSUALLY 'ARSH ON US. ANYWAY, WHAT DID YER WANT TER TALK TER ME ABOUT?

ARTHUR

IT WAS MARY AR ACTUALLY WANTED TER TALK TER YER ABOUT. AR 'AVE NOTICED THAT YER TWO 'AVE BEEN SPENDIN' A LOT OF TIME TOGETHER. DO YER FIND THE TIME TER DO MUCH BESIDES YOWER EDUCATION?

COOK

WE GO FOR WALKS IN TH' COUNTRYSIDE TOGETHER WHEN WE CAN FIND
TH' TIME, BUT APART FROM THAT WE DUNNA DO MUCH.

ARTHUR

YER COULD GO SWIMMIN' TOGETHER IN TH' LOCAL POOLS. MARY LOVES
SWIMMIN'.

COOK

SWIMMIN'? SPORT INNA REALLY SOMETHIN' AR FANCY.

ARTHUR

NOR ME REALLY. I PREFER TH' GAME OF KINGS.

(COOK LOOKS AT ARTHUR WITH CONFUSION)

CHESS.

COOK

AR 'AVE NEVER 'EARD CHESS BEIN' CALLED THAT BEFORE. IT IS A
TERM AR AM UNFAMILIAR WITH.

ARTHUR

PER'APS, WHEN YER AND MARY 'AVE FINISHED SWIMMING AR CAN TEACH
YER 'OW TER PLAY.

COOK

PER'APS, AYE.

(COOK RETURNS TO WORK)

(EXEUNT)

ACT I

SCENE 5

(1883. ENTER COOK AND MARY WALKING TOGETHER TOWARDS SHENTON'S HOUSE.)

MARY

DO YOU EVER THINK ABOUT LIFE BEYOND THE COAL FIELDS OF STAFFORDSHIRE?

COOK

SOMETIMES. SOMETIMES I DREAM ABOUT WHAT LIFE WOULD BE LIKE BEYOND THIS LITTLE TOWN, FREE OF THE COLLIERIES 'ERE IN SILVERDALE.

MARY

YOU MAKE IT SOUND AS IF SILVERDALE IS A BAD PLACE.

COOK

NO… I MEANT THAT THE WORLD MUST BE SO BEAUTIFUL BEYOND SILVERDALE. THIS PLACE WILL ALWAYS BE CLOSE TO ME 'EART, BUT I WANT TO KNOW MORE ABOUT TH' WORLD AND I FEAR THIS IS SOMETHIN' I CANNOT DO IN TH' CONFINES OF OUR 'UMBLE MINING VILLAGE.

MARY

JOSEPH, IF YOU WERE TO GO ON THIS PERSONAL QUEST OF DISCOVERY, WOULD I BE ABLE TO COME WITH YOU? I MUST SAY I HAVE GROWN RATHER FOND OF YOU DURING OUR TIME SPENT TOGETHER.

(TAKES COOK'S HAND)

COOK

IF GOD'S DIVINE PLAN INVOLVES US BEING TOGETHER, WHAT COULD WE DO? WHERE COULD WE GO? TH' POSSIBILITIES APPEAR A LITTLE TOO ENDLESS TO ME.

MARY

YOU KNOW, WE MAY NOT BE LIMITED IN OUR OPTIONS. WE COULD GO TO THE COLONIES. I HAVE ALWAYS WANTED TO SEE WHAT BRITISH LIFE IS LIKE OUTSIDE THE CONFINES OF OUR OWN ISLAND NATION.

COOK

'OW SO? THIS SORT OF DECISION IS NOT ONE THAT CAN BE MADE LIGHTLY. WE ARE TALKIN' ABOUT A LIFE CHANGIN' DECISION 'ERE. NOT 'ELP WITH EDUCATION.

MARY

ARE YOU NOT GRATEFUL FOR THE HELP I HAVE GIVEN YOU?

COOK

I AM MARY, I AM. AND I AM SORRY FOR SUGGESTIN' THAT I WAS NOT. I 'AVE ENJOYED EVERY MOMENT WE 'AVE SPENT TOGETHER SINCE WE FIRST MET.

MARY

REALLY?

COOK

YES. EVERYTHIN' YOU 'AVE DONE TO 'ELP ME ADVANCE ME STUDIES, I AM TRULY IN YOUR DEBT FOR.

MARY

I HAVE HAD PRACTICE WITH MY BROTHERS. I HELPED THEM TO READ AND WRITE AS I HAVE WITH YOU, BUT YOU ARE A MUCH MORE RECEPTIVE LEARNER THAN THEY ARE.

COOK

I TOLD YOU, I 'AVE A PASSION FOR KNOWLEDGE.

MARY

I NOTICED. IT IS A VERY IMPRESSIVE ATTRIBUTE TO HAVE.

COOK

QUITE. NEVERTHELESS I DO NOT SEE ANY FEASIBLE REASON TO LEAVE BRITAIN AT THIS TIME FOR THE COLONIES, DESPITE HAVING A FASCINATION WITH THEM MYSELF.

MARY

DO NOT BE SO SURE JOSEPH. ONE OF MY OLDER BROTHERS EMIGRATED TO NEW SOUTH WALES SEVERAL YEARS AGO. HE SENDS ME LETTERS SOMETIMES.

(*LAUGHS*)

YOU KNOW, FROM THE WAY HE TALKS ABOUT THE PLACE, HE MAKES IT SOUND LIKE THE BEST THING THAT EVER HAPPENED TO HIM.

COOK

THEN PERHAPS WE COULD START A FUTURE THERE. BUT UNTIL ME DEBT OF PROMISE IS REPAID TO ME FAMILY, I CANNOT GO WITH YOU.

MARY

FOR THE TIME BEING THEN, OUR FUTURE IS NOW, HERE IN SILVERDALE.

(ENTER SHENTON)

SHENTON

AH BROTHER COOK, SISTER MARY, THERE YOU ARE. ARTHUR AND I HAVE BEEN WAITING FOR YOU.

MARY

SORRY MR SHENTON.

SHENTON

DO NOT WORRY SISTER MARY, JUST TRY NOT TO BE LATE NEXT WEEK.
GO ON THROUGH.

(EXIT MARY - SHENTON STOPS COOK)

SHENTON

BROTHER COOK, MAY I HAVE A WORD WITH YOU?

COOK

OF COURSE.

SHENTON

OVER THE PAST COUPLE OF YEARS I HAVE WATCHED YOU EVOLVE FROM
THE SCARED CHILD YOU ONCE WERE, INTO THE CONFIDENT MAN I SEE
STANDING BEFORE ME NOW.

COOK

THANK YOU MR SHENTON, BUT TRUTHFULLY I COULD NOT 'AVE DONE ANY
OF THIS WITHOUT MARY.

SHENTON

I THOUGHT SHE MAY HAVE HAD A HAND IN HELPING YOU OUT. HER
DEDICATION TO WORK IS SIMPLY EXCEPTIONAL.

COOK

YES, NOT 'AS SHE ONLY BEEN ABLE TO 'ELP ME WITH ME EDUCATION,
BUT ALSO WITH ME CONFIDENCE.

SHENTON

OH YES? WHAT ARE YOU CURRENTLY LEARNING ABOUT?

COOK

I GENERALLY TEND TO LEARN ABOUT ME INTERESTS, AND AT TH'
MOMENT I AM INTERESTED IN TRADE UNIONS.

SHENTON

AH, AN INTERESTING TOPIC FOR A MINER SUCH AS YOURSELF. THOUGH
I FIND IT TO BE A LITTLE TOO POLITICAL FOR MY TASTE.

COOK

A SHAME. I 'OPED TO TALK ABOUT IT AT TH' MEETIN'.

SHENTON

I THINK THERE IS SOMEONE YOU NEED TO MEET, DR J MELLOR. HE
RUNS A DEBATING SOCIETY, WHICH I THINK YOU WOULD BENEFIT
HIGHLY FROM.

COOK

THANK YOU MR SHENTON.

SHENTON

THINK NOTHING OF IT MY BROTHER. THE GIFT I SEE IN YOU IS THE
HUNGER FOR KNOWLEDGE, AND THE DESIRE TO SHARE THAT KNOWLEDGE
WITH THE WORLD. THAT IS WHY I HAVE DECIDED TO MAKE YOU AN
HONORARY PREACHER.

(JOSEPH IS TOO SHOCKED TO SPEAK - ENTER MARY)

MARY

IS EVERYTHING ALRIGHT? YOU TWO HAVE BEEN TALKING FOR QUITE A
WHILE.

28

SHENTON

YES SISTER MARY, OUR CONVERSATION HAS BECOME A LITTLE LENGTHY.
IS ARTHUR MAKING THE TEA?

MARY

HE IS. HE ALSO TOLD ME THAT WE ARE NOW READY TO START. JOSEPH?

COOK

I 'AVE JUST BEEN MADE AN 'ONORARY PREACHER.

MARY

THAT IS FANTASTIC NEWS!

SHENTON

IT IS INDEED SISTER MARY. YOU TWO MAKE QUITE AN INFLUENTIAL
COUPLE. BOTH OF YOU SEEK TO HELP THE PEOPLES OF THE WORLD, YET
THE DIFFERENCE BETWEEN YOU IS THAT YOU SISTER MARY HELP WITH
ACTIONS, WHEREAS BROTHER COOK CHOOSES TO HELP WITH WORDS.

COOK

YES! WE COULD REALLY MAKE A DIFFERENCE IN TH' WORLD IF WE WORK
TOGETHER.

(JOSEPH AND MARY TAKE EACH OTHERS HANDS)

SHENTON

SHALL WE BEGIN THEN?

(EXEUNT)

ACT I

SCENE 6

(ARTHUR IS ONSTAGE ALONG WITH HIS FELLOW MINERS OUTSIDE THE MINE. THEY ARE BRANDISHING PLACARDS AND CHANTING SLOGANS.)

MINERS

(CALL AND RESPONSE WITH ARTHUR LEADING REPEAT IN UNISON UNTIL ARTHUR SETTLES THE MINERS)

OUR WORK, OUR LIFE!

NO PAY, WE STRIFE!

ARTHUR

WE CANNA ALLOW OUR WAY OF LIFE TER BE TAKEN AWAY FROM US LIKE THIS. THIS IS OUR LIFE, THIS IS WHAT WE LIVE FOR!

MINERS

(CHEERING)

ARTHUR

IF TH' MAYOR WUNNA RENEW TH' LEASE ON THE COLLIERIES, THEN WE SHALL NOT REST UNTIL 'E GIVES IN TER OUR DEMANDS!

(ARTHUR BEGINS TO RALLY THE MINERS, CHANTING SLOGANS.) (ENTER COOK)

COOK

ARTHUR!

(ARTHUR FAILS TO HEAR COOK OVER THE CHANTING)

ARTHUR!

(ARTHUR AGAIN FAILS TO HEAR COOK OVER THE CHANTING. COOK GRABS ARTHUR.)

ARTHUR!

30

ARTHUR

WHAT!?

COOK

WHAT IN TH' NAME OF THE LORD IS GOIN' ON 'ERE? AND 'OW ON EARTH DID YER GET THAT BLACK EYE?

ARTHUR

WHAT DOES IT LOOK LIKE JOSEPH? THE COLLIERIES OF SILVERDALE ARE UNDER ATTACK! OUR VERY WAY OF LIFE IS BEIN' THREATENED!

COOK

IS THERE ANY NEED TO GET SO WORKED UP ABOUT IT THOUGH? SINCE WHEN 'AVE YOU BEEN A REVOLUTIONARY MAN?

ARTHUR

(CHUCKLES)

YER REALLY 'AVE NO IDEA WHAT IS 'APPENING DO YER JOSEPH?

COOK

I MUST ADMIT, LATELY I 'AVE BEEN A LITTLE DISTANT DUE TO ME STUDIES, BUT THIS IS NOT YOU MY FRIEND.

ARTHUR

JOSEPH, I CAN EXPLAIN. WALK WITH ME AND I SHALL TELL YER EVERYTHIN'.

(ARTHUR AND COOK WALK TOGETHER. THE MINERS MOVE TO THE OPPOSITE SIDE OF THE STAGE.)

RECENTLY, TH' BUTTY MEN 'AVE BEEN PUSHIN' TH' MINERS A LITTLE TOO 'ARD, AND THIS 'AS BEEN AGGRAVATIN' NOT ONLY ME, BUT TH' REST OF TH' MINERS AS WELL.

31

COOK

ARTHUR, I THINK YOU CAN TAKE A LITTLE 'ARDSHIP. IF THAT WERE NOT TH' CASE WE WOULD NOT BE WORKIN' 'ARD IN TH' MINE FOR COAL.

ARTHUR

AR 'ATNA FINISHED YET JOSEPH. BEIN' ABSENT FOR A WEEK CAN 'AVE ITS CONSEQUENCES, ME FRIEND. A LOT CAN 'APPEN IN THIS SHORT SPACE OF TIME.

COOK

ALRIGHT THEN, TELL ME EVERYTHIN'.

ARTHUR

(*WHISPERED TONE*)

TH' BUTTY MEN 'AVE BEEN MUCH MORE BRUTAL AND UNFORGIVIN' LATELY. WE 'AVE LEARNED NOW THAT THIS IS BECAUSE OF A DIRECT ORDER FROM MAYOR STANIER. AN ORDER WHICH 'E THOUGHT WOULD INCREASE TH' PRODUCTION OF COAL.

COOK

SURELY IT CANNOT BE THAT BAD.

ARTHUR

WELL, WHEN TH' BUTTY TELLS YER STRAIGHT TO YOWER FACE THAT EVERY DROP OF SWEAT, BLOOD, EVERY OUNCE OF FLESH BELONGS TO 'IM. THAT IS WHEN YOWER SPIRIT BEGINS TER BREAK. AND THAT IS 'OW AR GOT ME BLACK EYE.

(*JOSEPH LOOKS STUNNED*)

AR WUZ STANDIN' UP FOR ME FELLOW MINERS. WE WUNNA ACCEPT IT ANY LONGER. AND WHEN AR TRIED TER STAND UP TER TH' BUTTY MAN 'IMSEN, 'E DID THIS TER ME.

COOK

I NEVER THOUGHT CONDITIONS WOULD GET THIS BAD. IN TH' MINE
CONDITIONS ARE ALREADY AWFUL, BUT THIS. THIS IS ONE STEP AWAY
FROM BECOMING SLAVERY.

ARTHUR

IF YOWER FAETHER WUZ STILL 'ERE, 'E WOULD 'AVE NEVER LET THIS
'APPEN. 'E WAS TH' BEST BUTTY MAN A MINER COULD ASK FOR. 'E
TREATED US AS IF WE WERE 'UMAN BEIN'S. 'E KNEW OUR LIMITS.

COOK

AND YOU SAY THIS IS ALL ON TH' ORDERS OF MAYOR STANIER?

ARTHUR

AYE.

COOK

PERHAPS I SHOULD PREPARE A SERMON SPEAKIN' OUT AGAINST 'IM. I
SHALL TALK TO MR SHENTON ABOUT TH' MATTER ARTHUR. WORRY NOT ME
FRIEND, WE SHALL FIND A WAY.

ARTHUR

OH JOSEPH, AR REALLY WISH IT ENDED THERE. AR REALLY WISH OUR
PROBLEMS ENDED REET THERE BUT THERE IS MORE.

COOK

GO ON.

ARTHUR

AFTER STANIER ORDERED TH' BUTTIES TER INCREASE TH' PRODUCTION
OF COAL 'E MUST 'AVE SEEN THAT 'IS PLAN WUZ FAILIN', SO 'E 'AS
REFUSED TER RENEW TH' LEASE OF TH' COLLIERIES. 'E IS
DESTROYIN' EVERYTHIN' YOWER FAETHER FOUGHT SO 'ARD TER BUILD.

COOK

WHAT?!

ARTHUR

STANIER REFUSED TER RENEW TH' LEASE OF TH' COLLIERIES. AND
BECAUSE OF THAT, OUR WAGES 'AVE PLUMMETED TER A LEVEL AT WHICH
WE CAN BARELY LIVE! FOR TH' SAKE OF ALL THAT IS 'OLY JOSEPH,
MOST OF US ARE TURNIN' TER POACHIN' JUST SO WE CAN FEED
OURSEN!

(ARTHUR SEES COOK GRIMACING WITH RAGE)

JOSEPH? ARE YER OW RITE?

COOK

I THOUGHT THIS WAS A SIMPLE MATTER OF RIGHT AND WRONG.

ARTHUR

IF IT INNA A MATTER OF RIGHT AND WRONG, THEN WHAT IS IT? MAYOR
STANIER IS FORCIN' IMMORALITY INTER OUR LIVES. 'E IS TURNING
US INTER CRIMINALS, SOMETHIN' AR WOULD RATHER NOT WANT TO BE.

(COOK PLACES HIS HAND ON ARTHUR'S SHOULDER)

COOK

THIS IS NOW A PERSONAL MATTER ARTHUR. THIS MAN IS NOT JUST
ATTACKIN' THE MINERS, 'E IS ATTACKIN' ME AS WELL. I MADE A
PROMISE THAT I WOULD TAKE CARE OF ME FAMILY, AND STANIER IS
NOW TRYIN' TO DESTROY OUR LEGACY. NOW I WILL NOT STAND IDLY BY
WHILE ME BROTHERS AND SISTERS SUFFER AT THE HANDS OF A GREEDY
POLITICIAN!

ARTHUR

THANK YER JOSEPH. IF YER EVER NEED ANY 'ELP, AR AM 'ERE FOR
YER.

COOK

TH' FIRST THING WE NEED TO DO IS MAKE PEOPLE AWARE OF WHAT IS 'APPENING. I SHALL PREPARE A SERMON, AND SPEAK TO TH' PEOPLE OF SILVERDALE. WE NEED TO REACH OUT TO OUR COMMUNITY ARTHUR, BUT I CANNOT DO THIS ALONE. I WANT YOU TO 'ELP ME WRITE THIS SERMON, SO THE PEOPLE CAN EXPERIENCE FIRST-'AND WHAT IS GOIN' ON.

ARTHUR

AR 'ATNA BEEN GOOD AT WRITIN' SPEECHES, BUT AR WILL TRY ME HARDEST.

COOK

THAT IS SOMETHIN' I CAN 'ELP YOU WITH. COME WITH ME ARTHUR.

(EXEUNT)

ACT I

SCENE 7

(ENTER COOK AND MARY TO A CROWD OF PEOPLE OUTSIDE. ARTHUR, SHENTON AND MARGARET COOKE ARE AMONG THEM. COOK TAKES THE PODIUM AND MARY JOINS THE CROWD.)

COOK

MY FRIENDS, IT IS GOOD TO SEE SO MANY OF YOU GATHERED 'ERE IN WHAT IS PERHAPS ONE OF SILVERDALE'S DARKEST 'OURS. I 'AVE ASKED TO SPEAK WITH YOU TODAY BECAUSE THERE IS AN EVIL GROWIN' IN THE 'EART OF OUR DEAR LITTLE VILLAGE.

PERSON 1

EVIL? IN SILVERDALE?

PERSON 2

YER MUST BE JOKIN'! THIS IS NOTHIN' BUT USELESS CHUNTER!

ARTHUR

'OLD YER NOISE! THIS IS AN ISSUE THAT AFFECTS ALL OF US 'ERE!

COOK

THANK YOU ARTHUR. AND AS ME BROTHER 'AS SO WELL PUT, THIS IS AN ISSUE THAT AFFECTS US ALL. YOU MAY NOT KNOW IT NOW, BUT YOU WILL SOON ENOUGH BECAUSE TH' BACKBONE OF OUR COMMUNITY IS UNDER THREAT.

(GASPS AND WHISPERING FROM CROWD)

I AM TALKIN' ABOUT TH' SILVERDALE COLLIERIES. TH' CONDITIONS AT TH' MINES 'AVE ALWAYS BEEN BAD. I KNOW THIS BECAUSE I 'AVE WORKED THERE MYSELF, AND I KNOW MOST OF YOU 'AVE AS WELL. BUT NOW MAYOR STANIER PROPOSES TO ENFORCE CRUEL AND UNFAIR CONDITIONS UPON TH' MEN IN WHAT SEEMS TO ME A FUTILE EFFORT TO INCREASE TH' PRODUCTION OF COAL.

36

PERSON 2

WHY SHOULD I CARE? CLOSIN' TH' MINES 'AS GOT NOTHIN' TER DO
WITH ME. I WORK FOR TH' SCHOOL.

COOK

THEN AS AN EDUCATED MAN YOU SHOULD BE ABLE TO UNDERSTAND THAT
THIS AFFECTS EVERYONE. WHETHER YOU WORK IN TH' MINES OR NOT,
TH' ECONOMY OF SILVERDALE IS FOUNDED ON TH' PRODUCTION OF
COAL. YOU SHOULD CARE BECAUSE WITHOUT COAL IT IS IMPOSSIBLE
FOR ANYONE TO LIVE A STABLE LIFESTYLE.

PERSON 1

TH' MINERS NEED TER GET BACK TER WORK THEN.

PERSON 3

NO! WE WUNNA ALLOW THIS INJUSTICE TER CONTINUE! WE MUST
PROTEST AGAINST TH' MAYOR!

PERSON 1

PROTEST AGAINST TH' MAYOR? WHY? 'E IS OUR PROVIDER, AND 'E 'AS
KEPT THIS COMMUNITY IN GOOD CONDITION FOR MANY YEARS NOW.

COOK

MAKE NO MISTAKE MY FRIENDS. MAYOR STANIER 'AS DONE SOME GOOD
THINGS FOR OUR LITTLE VILLAGE, BUT THESE CONDITIONS AT TH'
MINES WILL NOT ENCOURAGE TH' WORKERS TO WORK ANY 'ARDER. IF WE
WANT PRODUCTION OF COAL TO INCREASE, THEN WE SHOULD DO EXACTLY
THE OPPOSITE.

PERSON 2

THAT IS RIDICULOUS! IF TH' MINERS WORK 'ARDER TH' AMOUNT OF
COAL PRODUCED WILL INCREASE. WE MUST ENCOURAGE TH' MINERS TER
WORK FASTER. IF YER WANT AN 'ORSE TER RUN FAST, YER WHIP 'IM
AND 'E RUNS.

COOK

DO NOT LISTEN TO THIS MAN. BY TREATIN' TH' MINERS AS FELLOW 'UMAN BEINGS, WHO 'AVE LIMITS AND BOUNDARIES RATHER THAN ANIMALS, WE CAN ENSURE A FAST AND 'EALTHY PRODUCTION OF COAL. ME FATHER WILLIAM COOK, A FORMER BUTTY MAN KILLED IN THE MINES UNDERSTOOD THIS BETTER THAN ANYONE. FRIENDS, 'E TAUGHT ME THAT WORK IS TH' RENT ONE PAYS FOR LIFE. THAT THROUGH 'ARD WORK, WE CAN ACHIEVE SUCCESS.

PERSON 2

LISTEN TO YERSEN YER 'YPOCRITE! DID YER NOT SAY THAT THESE MEN ARE WORKIN' TH' MINERS TOO 'ARD?

COOK

THIS IS TRUE. AT FIRST, WHAT I SAY TO YOU ALL MAY SEEM A LITTLE 'YPOCRITICAL. BUT THESE MEN ARE NOT ALLOWIN' TH' MINERS TO WORK TO TH' BEST OF THEIR POTENTIAL, THEREFORE THEY ARE DESTINED TO FAIL AT THEIR LIVELIHOODS.

(BOOING AND JEERING FROM THE CROWD)

PEACE, PEACE ME FRIENDS. YOUR QUARREL IS NOT WITH ME, BUT RATHER WITH MAYOR STANIER. 'E IS RESPONSIBLE FOR THESE 'EINOUS ACTIONS UNDERTAKEN BY TH' BUTTY MEN. FURTHERMORE TO COVER 'IS TRACKS 'E IS NOW AIMING TO CLOSE TH' SILVERDALE COLLIERIES. 'E IS TH' REASON WHY MANY PEOPLE ARE LIVING AT THIS VERY MOMENT IN POVERTY AND DESPAIR. 'E IS RESPONSIBLE FOR TH' LIVES OF TH' PEOPLE WHO ARE CURRENTLY STRIKING AT THE MINES. 'E IS TH' REASON WHY ME BROTHERS AND SISTERS ARE TURNIN' INTO CRIMINALS, SIMPLY IN ORDER TO FEED THEIR FAMILIES.

(MORE GASPS, WHISPERING FROM CROWD.)

POACHIN', THEFT, CRIME IS 'APPENIN' TO GOOD PEOPLE RIGHT NOW, ALL IN TH' NAME OF ONE MAN'S IGNORANCE AND GREED. 'E KNOWS NOTHIN' ABOUT OUR STRUGGLE! I 'AVE WORKED IN TH' MINES AND I BECAME STRONG. I BEGAN TO EDUCATE MYSELF, WITH TH' 'ELP OF A BEAUTIFUL WOMAN, AND I BECAME WISE. BUT KNOW THIS. THESE MEN SENT BY STANIER CARE NOT ABOUT US. THEY WOULD ALL RATHER SEE OUR TEMPLES SUFFER AND CRUMBLE IN TH' NAME OF PROFIT. I SAY THAT WE MUST JOIN TOGETHER; MINERS, VILLAGERS, EVERYONE, AND WE MUST TAKE TH' FIGHT TO STANIER! WHO WILL STAND WITH ME?

(MARY, ARTHUR, SHENTON, MARGARET COOKE STAND UP.)

MARY, ARTHUR, SHENTON, MARGARET COOKE

WE WILL BROTHER JOSEPH!

(COOK PAUSES TO SURVEY CROWD. ONE BY ONE THEY STAND UP.)

COOK

THANK YOU, FRIENDS. THANK YOU ONE AND ALL. AS OF THIS MOMENT TH' CAMPAIGN AGAINST TH' MAYOR BEGINS. WE SHALL TAKE TH' FIGHT TO HIM AND SAVE OUR COMMUNITY!

(CLAPPING FROM THE CROWD. DISPERSE AND EXEUNT CROWD. MARY, SHENTON, ARTHUR AND MARGARET COOKE REMAIN.)

MARY

THAT WAS AMAZING JOSEPH. I HAVE NEVER SEEN YOU DO ANYTHING LIKE THAT BEFORE. WHERE ON EARTH DID YOU LEARN TO GIVE SPEECHES SUCH AS THIS?

COOK

I CANNOT TAKE FULL CREDIT. ARTHUR GAVE ME SOME 'ELP WITH THE FINER DETAILS.

MARY

REALLY? I NEVER KNEW YOU HAD THAT KIND OF PASSION ABOUT ANYTHING ARTHUR.

SHENTON

NOR DID I MY BROTHER. IT WAS SOMETHING VERY SPECIAL.

ARTHUR

WE WORKED ON TH' SPEECH TOGETHER BECAUSE THIS IS AN ISSUE THAT DEEPLY AFFECTS US BOTH. THIS IS SOMETHIN' WE NEED TO DO.

                            COOK

BY CLOSIN' TH' MINES, STANIER IS NOT ONLY AFFECTIN' OUR
LIFESTYLES, 'E IS ALSO INSULTING EVERYTHIN' ME FATHER FOUGHT
TO BUILD AT TH' COLLIERIES. I WILL NOT STAND IDLY BY AND LET
              HIM DESTROY TH' LEGACY OF ME FAMILY.

                           ARTHUR

AR RECKON 'E NEEDS TER BE 'UMBLED. AND THEN FOLLOWED UP WITH A
                   KICK UP THE BACKSIDE!

                          (LAUGHS)

                            MARY

ALLOW ME TO HELP YOU JOSEPH. THIS COULD BE OUR CHANCE TO MAKE
         REAL CHANGE FOR THE GOOD OF THE PEOPLE TOGETHER.

                            COOK

I 'AD A FEELING YOU MIGHT WANT TO 'ELP, AND I WOULD NOT 'AVE
IT ANY OTHER WAY MARY. YOU 'AVE BEEN AT MY SIDE FOR MANY YEARS
    AND 'ELPED ME THROUGH ME DARKEST 'OURS. I CANNOT REALLY
                   IMAGINE LIFE WITHOUT YOU.

                            MARY

        THANK YOU JOSEPH, THAT IS SO TOUCHING.

                            COOK

    YES. BUT BEFORE WE EMBARK ON WHAT WE NEED TO DO FOR
   SILVERDALE, THERE IS SOMETHIN' I NEED TO DO FOR YOU.

                         (KNEELS)

WOULD YOU DO ME TH' GRACIOUS 'ONOUR OF NOT ONLY BEIN' AT MY
        SIDE AS ME PARTNER, BUT ALSO AS ME WIFE?

                     (MARY TEARS UP)

                            40

MARY

YES JOSEPH. YES I WILL MARRY YOU.

(JOSEPH AND MARY GET EXCITED. THEY EMBRACE EACH OTHER THEN KISS.)

NOTHING WOULD MAKE ME HAPPIER.

(EXIT ALL BUT SHENTON)

SHENTON

FOR THERE TO BE A WEDDING, NOW OF ALL TIMES IS WHEN WE NEED IT MOST. A STEP BACK FROM THE PERILS AND TRAUMA WHICH THE WORLD BESTOWS UPON US. AND WITH THAT I WAIT UNTIL THE DAY WHEN MY BEST AND BRIGHTEST WILL JOIN, HAND IN HAND, TOGETHER.

(EXEUNT)

ACT I

SCENE 8

(SHENTON AND ARTHUR ARE ONSTAGE IN THE CHURCH OF THE PRIMITIVE METHODISTS.)

ARTHUR

IS EVERYTHIN' READY MR SHENTON?

SHENTON

OF COURSE, BROTHER ARTHUR.

(ENTER COOK)

ARTHUR

MIGHT AR SAY, AR THINK BOTH OF YER WILL BE VERY 'APPY TOGETHER. YER MAKE TH' PERFECT COUPLE.

COOK

VERY LIKE TH' KING AND QUEEN ON A CHESS BOARD EH?

ARTHUR

THERE IS NO DOUBT THAT MARY CAN BE A FEARSOME WOMAN WHEN SHE WANTS TER BE.

COOK

BUT THAT IS ONE OF TH' MANY REASONS WHY I LIKE 'ER ARTHUR. SHE IS SMART, STRONG WILLED AND VERY AFFIRMATIVE. SHE IS DEFINITELY MY QUEEN.

(COOK EMBRACES THEM BOTH AND THEN SMILES AS MARY ENTERS. COOK AND MARY ARE UNITED AT THE ALTAR. SHENTON IS CONDUCTING THE SERVICE, ARTHUR IS BY COOK. MARGARET COOKE IS SAT IN THE CROWD.)

SHENTON

WELCOME EVERYONE TO A MOST BEAUTIFUL OCCASION. WE HAVE COME TOGETHER AT THIS MOMENT TO CELEBRATE THE MARRIAGE OF TWO VERY BRIGHT, VERY LOVELY PEOPLE. BROTHER JOSEPH COOK AND SISTER MARY TURNER. I UNDERSTAND THAT BEFORE YOU ARE WED, BROTHER COOK WOULD LIKE TO SAY A FEW WORDS.

(SHENTON TURNS TO COOK)

COOK

OF COURSE.

(COOK TURNS TO MARY, BOWS HIS HEAD THEN LOOKS HER IN THE EYES.)

MARY. YOU ALLOWED ME TO FIND COURAGE IN MESELF. AND FOR THAT I AM MORE THAN GRATEFUL. YOU BRING OUT THE BEST IN ME, AS WELL AS OTHER PEOPLE. AND THIS IS WHY I LOVE YOU.

(MARY SMILES)

SHENTON

IF THERE ARE NO OBJECTIONS, WITHOUT ANY FURTHER ADO, I NOW PRONOUNCE YOU, BROTHER AND SISTER OF THE METHODIST CHURCH OF SILVERDALE, MAN AND WIFE!

(EXCITED CHEERING WHILE COOK KISSES MARY'S HAND)

COOK

NOW BEGINS ME NEW LIFE WITH YOU MRS COOK.

MARY

I AM DELIGHTED TO SHARE IT WITH YOU JOSEPH.

SHENTON

WHAT SHALL THE NEWLYWED COUPLE DECIDE TO DO WITH THEIR LIFE?

COOK

I MADE A PROMISE TO ME FAMILY TO KEEP THEM SAFE AND WELL. NOW THAT PROMISE IS ALL BUT FULFILLED. AND ALTHOUGH WE LOVE OUR DEAR LITTLE VILLAGE, IT IS LIKELY THAT WE WILL BE MOVIN' AWAY SOON. 'OWEVER, FOR NOW, OUR BUSINESS LIES WITH ENSURIN' A SAFE AND SECURE SOCIETY FOR SILVERDALE.

(APPLAUSE AND CONGRATULATIONS FROM ALL. EXIT MARGARET COOKE AND ARTHUR.)

MARY

YOU SHOW SUCH CONFIDENCE JOSEPH, WHEN YOU USED TO HAVE SUCH LITTLE FAITH IN YOURSELF. BUT WHAT CONFUSES ME IS WHERE YOU LEARNED HOW TO DO ALL OF THIS.

SHENTON

IT IS MAGNIFICENT TO SEE SUCH POTENTIAL BLOSSOMING.

(COOK LOOKS OVER AT SHENTON WHO SMILES BACK KNOWINGLY)

COOK

I CANNOT TAKE ALL THE CREDIT FOR WHAT I DO MARY. THE TRUTH IS, I 'AVE BEEN ABLE TO ACHIEVE SO MUCH BECAUSE OF YOU AND ME FRIENDS. NOW I BELIEVE WE HAVE WORK TO DO.

MARY

OH, HUSBAND. YOU CANNOT WORK ALL YOUR LIFE. COME AND CELEBRATE YOUR MARRIAGE FIRST.

COOK

OF COURSE ME LOVE.

(EXEUNT; COOK AND MARY (TOGETHER) AND SHENTON AFTERWARDS.)

ACT I

SCENE 9

(COOK AND MARY ARE ONSTAGE WITH CROWD. CROWD CONTINUOUSLY CHANTS.)

CROWD

WORK IS TH' RENT! WORK IS TH' RENT!

COOK

FOR TOO LONG 'AVE TH' MINERS OF SILVERDALE BEEN OPPRESSED BY TH' AUTHORITATIVE NATURE OF MAYOR STANIER! THE BUTTY MEN CONTINUOUSLY REFUSED TO ACKNOWLEDGE TH' DEMANDS FROM TH' MINERS THEMSELVES. BUT STANIER CANNOT IGNORE US FOREVER! IF WE ARE TO 'AVE OUR VOICES 'EARD, WE SHALL GO STRAIGHT TO 'IM.

(CHEERING FROM CROWD)

MARY

IF WORK IS THE RENT THAT PAYS FOR LIFE, THEN BY DENYING US THE BASIC RIGHTS WE DESERVE AS WORKERS, STANIER IS DENYING US OUR RIGHT TO LIVE.

(CHEERING FROM CROWD)

COOK

WORK IS OUR LIFE! IT FEEDS OUR FAMILIES! IT IS WHAT ALLOWS US TO SURVIVE, WITHOUT IT OUR LIVES BECOME MEANINGLESS. IT APPEARS OUR MAYOR DOES NOT REALISE THIS! 'E IS KILLIN' OUR WAY OF LIFE!

(CHEERING FROM CROWD)

CROWD

NO PAY! NO LIFE! NO WORK! WE STRIFE!

(REPEAT OVER AND OVER AGAIN UNTIL STANIER ENTERS)

STANIER

NOW THEN, NOW THEN, WHAT IS ALL THIS COMMOTION ABOUT?

(BOOING FROM CROWD)

COOK

'ERE APPEARS TH' BLIGHT UPON OUR COMMUNITY, AND YET 'E IS
OBLIVIOUS TO TH' PROBLEMS 'E IS CAUSIN'!

(STANIER LOOKS CONFUSED)

STANIER

YOU ARE OBVIOUSLY CONFUSED, YOUNG MAN. I HAVE BEEN DOING
NOTHING BUT GOOD THINGS FOR THIS VILLAGE IN THE PAST AND I
WILL CONTINUE TO DO GOOD THINGS IN THE FUTURE. NOW TELL ME
WHAT ALL THIS COMMOTION YOU ARE CAUSING IS ABOUT.

COOK

MAYOR STANIER, I, AS REPRESENTATIVE OF TH' MINERS OF
SILVERDALE, 'OLD YOU RESPONSIBLE FOR TH' DISGRACES YOU 'AVE
CAUSED IN THIS VILLAGE FOLLOWIN' YOUR REFUSAL TO RENEW TH'
LEASE OF TH' COLLIERIES. YOU ARE ROBBIN' US OF OUR WORK, AND
THEREFORE OUR LIVES!

CROWD

WORK IS TH' RENT! WORK IS TH' RENT!

STANIER

REALLY?

(TO CROWD)

SO THIS IS WHAT YOU THINK OF YOUR MAYOR? IS THIS WHAT YOU
THINK OF YOUR PROTECTOR?

(CROWD CHEERS)

MARY

YES IT IS MR MAYOR.

STANIER

AND WHO ARE YOU TO CHALLENGE ME?

MARY

I AM MARY COOK MR MAYOR.

STANIER

(*ASIDE*)

COOK?

MARY

I MAY BE A SMALL WOMAN, BUT I KNOW RIGHT FROM WRONG, AND I AM WILLING TO FIGHT FOR WHAT I KNOW IS RIGHT ALONGSIDE MY HUSBAND, JOSEPH COOK.

STANIER

JOSEPH COOK. I KNEW I RECOGNISED YOUR FAMILY NAME. I WOULD LIKE TO PERSONALLY SAY TO YOU NOW, IN FRONT OF ALL YOUR SUPPORTERS, THAT YOU HAVE BEEN THE BANE OF MY LIFE FOR THE PAST FEW MONTHS. BUT I WOULD ALSO LIKE YOU TO KNOW THAT I DO NOT THINK THAT YOU KNOW WHAT YOU ARE ACTUALLY DOING.

COOK

NO, I DO NOT THINK YOU KNOW WHAT YOU ARE DOIN' STANIER. YOU ARE PUSHING TH' GOOD MEN AND WOMEN OF THIS TOWN TO THEIR GRAVES. YOU ARE TURNING THEM INTO TH' VERY THINGS THEY 'ATE. YOU ARE CAUSIN' NOTHIN' BUT PROBLEMS FOR OUR COMMUNITY. PEOPLE ARE TURNIN' TO THEFT AND POACHING BECAUSE THEY ARE SIMPLY THAT DESPERATE FOR FOOD AND NOURISHMENT. AND IN TIMES SUCH AS THIS, WE WOULD LOOK TO OUR LEADER FOR HELP. THEN WE REMEMBER THAT HE IS TH' PESTILENCE THAT PLAGUES THIS VILLAGE!

(CHEERING FROM CROWD)

STANIER

HA. MR COOK, YOU ARE VERY FUNNY. I THINK YOU AND I NEED TO
HAVE A TALK ABOUT WHAT IS REALLY GOING ON IN THIS COMMUNITY.
STEP INTO MY OFFICE AND I SHALL EXPLAIN EVERYTHING.

COOK

MARY COMES WITH ME. SHE IS ME EQUAL IN THIS FIGHT.

STANIER

FINE. THIS WAY PLEASE MR AND MRS COOK.

(EXIT CROWD. STANIER LEADS THEM TO THE OTHER SIDE OF THE
STAGE.)

SO, MR JOSEPH COOK, WHERE WOULD YOU LIKE TO BEGIN NOW THAT WE
ARE PRIVATE ENOUGH TO HAVE A CIVILISED CONVERSATION?

COOK

MAYOR STANIER.

(STANIER POURS HIMSELF A DRINK)

STANIER

PLEASE. CALL ME FRANCIS MR COOK.

COOK

FRANCIS, YOU NEED TO UNDERSTAND. MINING IS ALL THAT MOST OF
TH' PEOPLE OF SILVERDALE 'AVE. WHEN YOU REFUSED TO RENEW TH'
LEASE ON TH' COLLIERIES, YOU STABBED TH' 'EART OF MANY A GOOD
PERSON.

MARY

AND NOW MR MAYOR, THE MINERS ARE REACHING OUT IN DESPERATION. PLEASE, YOU HAVE TO DO SOMETHING, THE LESS FORTUNATE THAN US ARE STARVING TO DEATH RIGHT NOW! DO YOU NOT CARE ABOUT THE PEOPLE OF SILVERDALE?

STANIER

OF COURSE I CARE MRS COOK. THAT IS WHY I DID NOT RENEW THE LEASE OF THE COLLIERIES.

COOK

WHAT?

STANIER

DESPITE WHAT YOU MAY BELIEVE MR COOK, I DO CARE ABOUT THE LIVES OF THESE PEOPLE.

COOK

I CANNOT BELIEVE THIS! 'OW CAN YOU EXPECT TO BE VIEWED AS A CARIN' INDIVIDUAL WHEN YOU 'AVE TAKEN SO MUCH FROM THE MINERS?

STANIER

I DID NOT TAKE ANYTHING FROM THEM MR COOK, IF ANYTHING THEY DID THIS TO THEMSELVES. WHAT YOU AND THEY DO NOT UNDERSTAND IS THAT BY STRIKING YOU ARE DRAINING YOUR OWN RESOURCES! HOW CAN MAN EXPECT TO SUPPORT HIMSELF IF HE HAS NO INCOME? I HAVE HAD NOTHING TO DO WITH THE ACTIONS OF YOUR PEOPLE JOSEPH. IF THEY CHOOSE TO BECOME CRIMINALS THEN SO BE IT, I WILL PURSUE THEM UNTIL I CATCH THEM AND THEN THEY WILL BE PROSECUTED TO THE FULL EXTENT OF THE LAW!

COOK

THIS IS DISGUSTING! THIS IS WHAT IT IS ALL ABOUT TO YOU. MONEY!

STANIER

OF COURSE IT IS ABOUT MONEY! WHAT DO YOU THINK WE USE TO BUY OUR FOOD, TO PAY FOR OUR CLOTHES, OUR MEDICINE, OUR EDUCATION?! I AM SORRY MR COOK, BUT I HAD NO CHOICE.

MARY

YOU ALWAYS HAVE A CHOICE MR MAYOR. WHERE ARE YOUR SENSE OF MORALS, YOUR DECENCY?

STANIER

WHEN YOU ARE THRUST INTO A POSITION OF POWER MRS COOK, SOMETIMES YOU HAVE TO FORGET SUCH THINGS IN ORDER TO MAKE THE CHOICES NO ONE ELSE CAN MAKE. THE RIGHT CHOICES.

COOK

WHAT IS RIGHT TO YOU THEN MR MAYOR?

STANIER

I TOLD YOU BOTH I HAD NO CHOICE. THE MARKET SURROUNDING COAL WAS PLUMMETING. IN ORDER TO PROTECT THE ASSETS OF THE INDUSTRY, NOT TO MENTION THE SURROUNDING MINES IN THE AREA, I HAD TO CLOSE THE SILVERDALE COLLIERIES. WITH THE MARKET IN CRISIS, I SIMPLY DO NOT HAVE THE MONEY TO RENEW THE LEASE AND PAY THE WAGES OF ALL THE WORKERS. I AM SORRY JOSEPH BUT THAT IS THE WAY THAT BUSINESS AND POLITICS WORK.

COOK

BUT… BUT… WHAT ABOUT TH' MINERS, WHAT ABOUT ME FRIENDS? YOU CANNOT JUST ABANDON THEM LIKE THIS.

STANIER

THEY ARE HUMAN BEINGS JOSEPH. EVENTUALLY THEY WILL GET OVER IT. THOUGH I CANNOT OPEN THE SILVERDALE COLLIERIES AGAIN WITHOUT THE NECESSARY FUNDING, YOU CAN ADVISE THAT THEY FIND NEW JOBS. PERHAPS INSTEAD OF LEADING THESE PEOPLE ON A FUTILE CRUSADE, YOU SHOULD EXPLAIN THAT TO THEM. THIS IS NOT THE END OF THE WORLD. BESIDES, LIKE ME, YOU ALSO LACK MONEY AND I THINK YOUR LITTLE PROTEST WILL NOT LAST VERY LONG WITHOUT RESOURCES. AS SOON AS THE MINERS BECOME TRULY DESPERATE, THEY WILL COME TO THEIR SENSES AND REALISE THAT THEY NEED WORK. OR WOULD YOU RATHER TELL THEM THAT YOURSELF?

COOK

MAY I 'AVE A MOMENT WITH ME WIFE PLEASE?

STANIER

OF COURSE MR COOK.

(EXIT STANIER)

MARY

WHAT ARE YOU THINKING JOSEPH?

COOK

(SIGHS)

STANIER IS RIGHT. 'E MAY BE A DESPICABLE MAN, BUT 'E IS RIGHT.

MARY

WE GOING TO GIVE INTO HIM? JUST LIKE THAT?

COOK

BELIEVE ME I DO NOT LIKE MAKIN' THIS DECISION ANY BETTER THAN YOU LIKE HEARIN' IT, BUT TH' ONLY ROLE STANIER 'AS 'AD IN THIS CATASTROPHE IS THAT 'E WAS UNABLE TO RENEW TH' LEASE. AND WE BECAME ENRAGED FOR THIS. NO, TH' BEST WAY FORWARD IS FOR TH' MINERS TO FIND NEW JOBS.

MARY

BUT WHAT WILL HAPPEN TO ARTHUR? WHAT WILL HAPPEN TO US?

COOK

DO NOT WORRY ME LOVE. WE CAN FIGURE SOMETHIN' OUT.

(ENTER STANIER)

STANIER

IS EVERYTHING ALRIGHT?

COOK

YES. ALTHOUGH I 'ATE TO ADMIT IT, YOU ARE RIGHT. I THOUGHT YOU WERE DESTROYING TH' LEGACY OF MY FATHER BY CLOSING TH' COLLIERIES, BUT NOW I SEE THAT WE ARE NOT SO DIFFERENT.

STANIER

HOW?

COOK

WE ARE BOTH MEN TRYING TO SURVIVE IN THIS WORLD'S CRUEL WILDERNESS.

STANIER

I AM GLAD YOU ARE FINALLY ABLE TO SEE MY POINT OF VIEW MR COOK. WILL YOU TELL THE MINERS OF THIS?

COOK

I SHALL. I THINK IT IS BEST IF I BREAK TH' NEWS IN PERSON TO THEM. WE WILL SEE OURSELVES OUT.

(COOK AND MARY BEGIN TO EXIT)

STANIER

MR COOK, MAY I HAVE A WORD WITH YOU?

COOK

OF COURSE. MARY, WILL YOU WAIT FOR ME OUTSIDE?

MARY

YES JOSEPH.

COOK

THANK YOU.

(EXIT MARY)

WHAT DO YOU WANT TO TELL ME?

STANIER

I WANT YOU TO KNOW THAT I HAVE A LOT OF RESPECT FOR YOU JOSEPH. I WORKED WITH YOUR FATHER FOR MANY YEARS, AND I CAN SEE HIS GOOD NATURE AND KEEN INTELLIGENCE IN YOU. YOU ARE A SMART MAN AND A GREAT LEADER, BUT UNLIKE YOUR FATHER YOU LACK NECESSARY WISDOM. WILLIAM KNEW THAT BEING A GOOD MAN WAS NEVER GOING TO BE ENOUGH. HE KNEW THAT IN ORDER TO SUCCEED AT ANYTHING, YOU HAVE TO FAIL FIRST. I REMEMBER HIM TELLING ME THAT IT IS AN INEVITABILITY OF LIFE. DO NOT FEEL DISAPPOINTED IN YOURSELF JOSEPH. YOUR FATHER WAS A WISE MAN, AND I HOPE YOU CAN USE HIS KNOWLEDGE TO MAKE SOMETHING OF YOURSELF IN THE FUTURE.

COOK

I SHALL FRANCIS, AND I SHALL STRIVE TO BECOME MORE LIKE ME
FATHER.

(ENTER MARY)

STANIER

GOOD LUCK JOSEPH, AND THANK YOU.

(EXIT STANIER)

MARY

ARE YOU ALRIGHT JOSEPH?

COOK

I FEEL SORROW FOR TH' MINERS MARY. I DO NOT WANT TO TELL THEM
WE FAILED BUT I MUST.

MARY

SOMETIMES THE TRUTH HURTS JOSEPH. BUT WE MUST GO ON
REGARDLESS.

COOK

BUT WHAT MUST I DO ABOUT TH' LEGACY MY FATHER LEFT BEHIND?

MARY

HE MUST HAVE BEEN A REMARKABLE MAN. BUT WHAT I THINK HE WOULD
WANT FOR US MOST IS TO CREATE A LEGACY OF OUR OWN.

(PAUSE)

MY BROTHER LIVES IN LITHGOW. PERHAPS YOU COULD LOOK FOR WORK
THERE.

COOK

I DID SAY IT WAS POSSIBLE OUR FUTURE COULD LIE IN THE
COLONIES. ARE THERE MANY JOBS IN LITHGOW?

MARY

IT IS A SMALL MINING COMMUNITY. WE CAN STAY WITH MY BROTHER
UNTIL WE HAVE ENOUGH MONEY FOR A PLACE OF OUR OWN.

COOK

THEN PERHAPS IT IS TIME. MY PROMISES HAVE BEEN FULFILLED AND
SO NOW WE CAN LEAVE FOR THE COLONIES AND START OUR OWN FUTURE.

(THEY SMILE AT EACH OTHER. EXEUNT)

ACT II

SCENE 1

(AUSTRALIA, 1893. ENTER COOK, LYNE, DEAKIN, FISHER AND OTHER POLITICIANS. MANY OF THEM ARE GATHERED AROUND A TABLE. COOK AND LYNE ARE SAT AT THE SIDE PLAYING A GAME OF CHESS.)

LYNE

CHECK. YOUR TURN JOSEPH.

(COOK SURVEYS THE BOARD THEN DECIDES HIS MOVE)

COOK

I MUST SAY WILLIAM, YOU ARE A SHREWD CHESS PLAYER. YOU CERTAINLY ARE CONFIDENT IN YOUR APPROACH. BUT MY KNIGHT TAKES YOUR CASTLE. I WOULD SAY THAT IS CHECKMATE.

LYNE

NOT SO FAST JOSEPH. IT IS OBVIOUS THAT YOU HAVE FORGOTTEN ABOUT MY QUEEN.

COOK

WHAT ABOUT IT? MY KING IS QUITE SAFE FROM HER.

LYNE

SHE IS FAR FROM SAFE MY FRIEND. MY BISHOP TAKES YOUR KNIGHT.

COOK

AND IN TURN I TAKE YOUR BISHOP WITH MY PAWN.

LYNE

A GRIEVOUS ERROR MY FRIEND.

(*LYNE MOVES FORWARD A PAWN*)

CHECKMATE. BECAUSE YOU TOOK MY BISHOP WITH YOUR PAWN, YOU FREED MY QUEEN TO TAKE UP THIS COLUMN. SO, BY MOVING MY PAWN FORWARD ONE SPACE, YOUR KING IS TRAPPED WITH NOWHERE TO GO.

COOK

I CAN JUST TAKE THE PAWN. HAVE YOU FORGOTTEN THAT WILLIAM?

LYNE

(*LAUGHS*)

THIS IS WHERE CHESS GETS INTERESTING JOSEPH. IF YOU TAKE MY PAWN, YOU MOVE YOUR KING INTO THE DIRECT PATH OF MY OTHER ROOK. AND THAT IS AN ILLEGAL MOVE. UNLESS YOU WISH TO HAVE YOUR KING TAKEN.

(*JOSEPH LOOKS STUNNED AT THE BOARD, REALISING HIS FRIEND IS RIGHT.*)

I BELIEVE THAT IS CHECKMATE.

COOK

YOU CERTAINLY HAVE TAKEN CONFIDENCE IN YOURSELF SINCE YOUR KNIGHTHOOD.

LYNE

BEING A KNIGHT COMMANDER HAS NOTHING TO DO WITH IT. ASSERTING YOURSELF WITH CONFIDENCE CAN MEAN THE DIFFERENCE BETWEEN LIFE AND DEATH IN POLITICS.

COOK

TOO TRUE. THOUGH I HAVE HAD SITUATIONS WHERE CONFIDENCE IS NOT ENOUGH TO SEE OUT THE DAY.

LYNE

YES. YOU HAVE TO BE THINKING THREE STEPS AHEAD OF YOUR OPPONENT AT ALL TIMES.

COOK

I SUPPOSE, YES. BUT THERE IS ALSO A QUESTION OF MORALITY. BEING A GOOD AND HONEST PERSON WILL ALWAYS ACT AS A BENEFIT.

LYNE

YES, WELL. I AM NOT SURE I AGREE WITH YOU THERE. SHALL WE JOIN THE OTHERS?

COOK

CERTAINLY.

(THEY WALK OVER AND JOIN THE REST OF THE POLITICIANS)

POLITICIAN (BARTON)

MY FELLOW PATRIOTS OF AUSTRALIA. WE ARE TRULY BLESSED UPON THIS DAY. TODAY WE HAVE THE OPPORTUNITY TO CREATE A UNIFIED NATION. A BETTER AUSTRALIA FOR ALL THE PEOPLES OF THIS COUNTRY. IF YOU WOULD ALL CARE TO LISTEN TO WHAT MR DEAKIN AND MR FISHER HAVE PROPOSED, WE CAN BEGIN.

DEAKIN

THANK YOU EDMUND. TODAY WE FORM THE FOUNDATIONS OF THE GOVERNMENT. OUR FUTURE PRINCIPLES WILL BE DECIDED HERE AND NOW, AND ALL OF YOU MEN HAVE BEEN INVITED HERE TODAY TO HELP US CREATE A COUNTRY FOUNDED IN STABILITY.

FISHER

QUITE RIGHT DEAKIN. LABOUR SEEKS TO HERALD AN AGE OF PROSPERITY, AND WE AIM TO GIVE BACK TO THE PEOPLE.

DEAKIN

WHICH IS WHY WE HAVE GATHERED. MOST OF YOU ONLY REPRESENT THE MINOR DIVISIONS OF THE LABOUR PARTY. OUR POLICIES ARE TO INVEST IN THE GROWTH AND DEVELOPMENT OF OUR NATION.

COOK

EXCUSE ME.

DEAKIN

YES MR COOK.

COOK

I AM ONLY CURIOUS BUT I WOULD LIKE TO KNOW HOW EXACTLY WE ARE GOING TO INVEST IN OUR NATION. GROWTH AND DEVELOPMENT ARE FINE TERMS, BUT I WOULD PREFER SOME KNOWLEDGE OF HOW WE ARE DOING THIS.

LYNE

SECONDED. WE CANNOT BE EXPECTED TO COMPLY WITH ANYTHING IF WE KNOW NOTHING ABOUT WHAT WE ARE AGREEING TO. FRANKLY, IT IS UNWISE.

FISHER

YOU ARE CORRECT LYNE. IT IS UNWISE.

DEAKIN

OUR PLAN IS TO PROVIDE STABLE JOBS FOR THE PEOPLE BY INCREASING TAXES ON OUR IMPORTS AND EXPORTS. I BELIEVE THAT WE MUST BE PROTECTIVE OF OUR ASSETS IF OUR ECONOMY IS TO GROW.

COOK

MR DEAKIN, PLEASE CORRECT ME IF I HAVE SOMEHOW FAILED TO UNDERSTAND, BUT HOW CAN WE EXPECT TO GROW AN ECONOMY IF WE ONLY FOCUS ON PROTECTING OUR ASSETS?

FISHER

ARE YOU SERIOUSLY SUGGESTING THAT WE SHOULD OPEN TRADE ROUTES OUTSIDE OF OUR OWN COUNTRY?

COOK

YES MR FISHER. I AM TALKING ABOUT MAKING THE TRADING MARKET FREE NOT JUST FOR US, BUT FOR OUR ALLIES AS WELL.

(LYNE GIVES COOK A DIRTY LOOK OF SHOCK)

POLITICIAN (REID)

SECONDED! THAT WAY WE WILL BENEFIT FROM LONG LASTING, STABLE RELATIONSHIPS WITH THEM.

FISHER

FREE TRADE WILL DESTABILISE THE VERY ECONOMY YOU HAVE BEEN SUMMONED TO HELP PROSPER, GENTLEMEN. WE SHALL LEAVE IT AT THAT.

COOK

NO, YOU ARE CLEARLY MISINFORMED ABOUT WHAT FREE TRADE CAN DO. IF WE HAVE GOOD RELATIONS WITH THE COUNTRIES AROUND US, THIS WILL LEAD TO MORE GROWTH AND DEVELOPMENT NOT ONLY WITHIN, BUT OUTSIDE OUR COUNTRY.

DEAKIN

PERHAPS, YOUNG COOK. I RESPECT YOUR BELIEFS, BUT AS MR FISHER HAS STATED, BY OPENING THE MARKET FREELY WE TAKE THE RISK OF DESTABILISING OUR ECONOMY. WHICH IS A RISK WE CANNOT AFFORD TO TAKE.

COOK

BUT…

DEAKIN

BY PROTECTING OUR OWN ASSETS, WE CAN CREATE JOBS HERE IN
AUSTRALIA.

(COOK STARES BEWILDERED AT DEAKIN. FISHER SNEERS AT COOK.)

THAT IS MY FINAL WORD COOK. THE FOCUS OF THE LABOUR PARTY
NEEDS TO BE ON THE AUSTRALIAN PEOPLE, NOT SCATTERED ACROSS THE
WORLD. ALL IN FAVOUR?

ALL BUT COOK, FISHER, LYNE, REID

AYE!

FISHER

(PAUSES)

AYE!

LYNE

AYE!

COOK

WILLIAM TELL ME YOU DO NOT BELIEVE IN THIS STUPID FALLACY.

LYNE

THIS STUPID FALLACY IS THE MOST LOGICAL WAY OF CREATING A
GOVERNMENT JOSEPH. WHAT YOU ASK OF THE LABOUR PARTY IS SIMPLY
UNREASONABLE.

(LYNE JOINS THE OTHERS. ONLY COOK AND REID ARE LEFT.)

COOK

SINCE I CANNOT CHANGE YOUR MINDS, WE SHALL FORM OUR OWN PARTY. WE SHALL STAY TRUE TO THE PRINCIPLES OF FREE TRADE AND A BETTER TOMORROW FOR ALL.

DEAKIN

IF THAT IS WHAT YOU WANT, THEN I WISH YOU WELL COOK.

(COOK AND DEAKIN SHAKE HANDS. EXIT COOK AND REID.)

FISHER

GENTLEMEN. GOVERNMENT ENSUES. WE HAVE WORK TO DO.

(EXEUNT)

ACT II

SCENE 2

(FOCUS SHIFTS TO A CONTEMPLATING COOK AT HIS DESK. THE COOK HOUSEHOLD, 1901. ENTER MARY.)

MARY

ARE YOU WRITING ANOTHER LETTER TO ARTHUR? IT HAS BEEN A WHILE SINCE WE HAVE HEARD FROM HIM.

COOK

NO, IT IS A LETTER TO JOHN.

MARY

MR SHENTON?

COOK

I NEVER HAD THE CHANCE TO THANK HIM PROPERLY FOR THE BIBLE HE GAVE ME. CAN YOU MAIL THE LETTER WHEN YOU NEXT HEAD INTO TOWN?

MARY

OF COURSE. NOW LET ME GO AND GET YOUR TEA.

(EXIT MARY. JOSEPH LOOKS INTO THE DISTANCE. ENTER GEORGE.)

GEORGE

IS EVERYTHING ALRIGHT FATHER? YOU SEEM A LITTLE DISTANT.

COOK

YES, GEORGE I AM FINE. BUT EVERY NOW AND THEN I THINK OF EVERYTHING I LEFT BEHIND IN ENGLAND. EVERYTHING I SACRIFICED TO MAKE IT TO THE COLONIES.

GEORGE

YOU HAVE TOLD ME THIS STORY ALREADY FATHER. YOU CAME HERE TO FIND WORK AFTER THE MINES CLOSED.

COOK

I NEVER TOLD YOU THE ENTIRE STORY MY BOY. YOU SEE, THE MINERS DID NOT TAKE WELL TO FINDING NEW JOBS. THEY BLAMED ME FOR THINGS THAT WERE BEYOND MY CONTROL. YOUR MOTHER AND I DID PLAN TO COME HERE ANYWAY, BUT WE BOTH FELT THE MOVE WAS BEST AFTER…

GEORGE

AFTER WHAT?

COOK

I FELT AS THOUGH I HAD FAILED THEM, SO I WANTED TO FORGET. WE WANTED TO START AGAIN SOMEWHERE NEW SO WE CAME TO AUSTRALIA.

GEORGE

IT DOES NOT SOUND AS THOUGH YOU FAILED THEM FATHER.

COOK

YOU WERE NOT THERE SON.

(PAUSE)

GEORGE

WAS THAT WHY YOU WENT INTO POLITICS?

COOK

NO, I STARTED AT THE MINES. YOUR UNCLE FOUND ME A JOB THERE, WHICH WAS WHERE I MET MY GOOD FRIEND WILLIAM LYNE. HE WAS THE ONE WHO CONVINCED ME TO MAKE THE TRANSITION TO POLITICS.

GEORGE

I HAVE HEARD YOU TALK ABOUT HIM. WHAT I DO NOT UNDERSTAND IS WHY YOU WERE FRIENDS WITH SOMEONE FROM THE OPPOSITION?

COOK

WHEN THE PARTY WAS FOUNDED THERE WAS LITTLE OPPOSITION. LYNE AND I HAD WORKED IN THE MINES FOR MANY YEARS AND THEN WE WORKED FOR THE AUSTRALIAN LABOUR PARTY.

(ENTER MARY WITH TEA)

BUT THERE WAS A MAJOR DISAGREEMENT SEVERAL YEARS AGO WHICH DIVIDED US ALL.

MARY

YOU HAD A DISAGREEMENT JOSEPH, THESE THINGS HAPPEN.

COOK

NOT LIKE THIS MARY. I WISH LYNE AND I COULD STILL BE FRIENDS, BUT I FEAR HE IS BEING CONSUMED BY HIS HATRED OF TRADE UNIONS.

GEORGE

WHAT HAPPENED TO HIM?

COOK

FISHER NEVER FORGAVE EITHER OF US FOR LEAVING THE PARTY, LET ALONE STARTING OUR OWN: THE FREE TRADERS AND THE PROTECTIONISTS, EACH TO RIVAL HIM. BUT I STAND BY MY ACTIONS TO THIS DAY.

(JOSEPH LOOKS OVER AT GEORGE. HE PLACES HIS HAND ON HIS SHOULDER.)

NEVER FORGET MY BOY. ALWAYS BE TRUE TO YOURSELF AND PERSEVERE. IT IS SOMETHING I HAVE TRIED TO DO ALL MY LIFE.

MARY

BUT NEITHER OF YOU WILL BE ABLE TO DO ANY OF IT WITHOUT A GOOD
NIGHT SLEEP.

(EXIT GEORGE AND MARY)

COOK

BIG DAY TOMORROW.

(EXEUNT)

ACT II

SCENE 3

(STAGE REOPENS TO SHOW THE AUSTRALIAN PARLIAMENT. MELBOURNE. ENTER COOK, LYNE, DEAKIN, FISHER, HUGHES AND OTHER POLITICIANS.)

DEAKIN

HEAR ME, HEAR ME! JOSEPH COOK OF THE FREE TRADERS HAS THE FLOOR.

COOK

THANK YOU MR PRIME MINISTER. NOW AS YOU KNOW, WE ARE STILL ONLY JUST BEGINNING TO DEVELOP AS A COUNTRY. OUR GOVERNMENT GROWS EVERY DAY AS MORE PEOPLE DECIDE TO TAKE AN INTEREST IN POLITICS.

FISHER

WHAT IS YOUR POINT COOK?

COOK

MY POINT MR FISHER, IS THAT WE SHOULD BEGIN TO THINK OF OURSELVES AS A COUNTRY WHO CAN COMPETE WITH THE REST OF THE WORLD. AND YET I AM STILL SEEING CASES OF WHAT I CONSIDER TO BE INSTITUTIONAL MALPRACTICE IN OUR COUNTRY. I REALISE WE ARE THE STEPPING STONE FOR A GREATER TOMORROW, BUT IN ORDER FOR US TO LIVE UP TO THAT NAME WE NEED TO FOLLOW THROUGH ON OUR PROMISES.

LYNE

SIT THIS MAN DOWN! HE IS NO POLITICIAN. HE IS ONLY A RAMBLING FOOL!

COOK

WHAT I AM TRYING TO SAY, LYNE, IS THAT WE MUST BEGIN TO PAY EACH AND EVERY MAN ACROSS THIS COUNTRY A FAIR AND DECENT WAGE FOR THE EFFORT THEY PUT INTO THEIR JOBS.

LYNE

THEY ARE PAID A DECENT WAGE COOK! PERHAPS YOU WOULD KNOW THIS IF YOU WERE REALLY AWARE OF THE SITUATION.

COOK

YOU SEE MY FRIENDS. THIS IS WHAT I MEAN. I PUT IT TO ALL OF YOU THAT MINISTER LYNE IS THE ONE WHO IS UNAWARE OF THE SITUATION.

LYNE

HOW DARE YOU QUESTION MY INTEGRITY COOK!

COOK

TAKE A LOOK AT REALITY LYNE. THERE ARE PEOPLE WHO ARE BEING MISTREATED BECAUSE OF YOUR BAD PRACTICES.

(LYNE IS SHOCKED)

LYNE

BAD PRACTICES? I AM A KNIGHT COMMANDER, THE MINISTER FOR TRADE AND CUSTOMS OF THIS GREAT NATION. I AM THE BEST MAN FOR THE JOB AND I WILL NOT TOLERATE SUCH INSUBORDINATION FROM A BACK BENCHER LIKE YOU!

COOK

I CANNOT FAULT YOU THERE LYNE. YOU HAVE A PRESTIGIOUS TITLE. YET IT IS WORTHLESS IF YOU FAIL TO DO YOUR JOB PROPERLY.

LYNE

COOK, YOU ARE TESTING MY PATIENCE!

DEAKIN

ORDER! WE WILL HAVE ORDER! MINISTER LYNE, LET COOK SPEAK. HE IS TRYING TO RAISE AN ISSUE.

COOK

THANK YOU PRIME MINISTER. MANY OF THE PLACES I HAVE WORKED AT IN THE PAST MAKE USE OF PROPER WAGES TO PAY THEIR WORKERS FOR THEIR EFFORTS. YET I HAVE ALSO WORKED WITH AND LED MEN WHO WERE NOT PAID IN ANY FORM OF CURRENCY, BUT RATHER WITH OBJECTS INSTEAD. IF WE ARE TO BE THE FOUNDATION FOR OUR COUNTRY, WE NEED TO START PAYING EVERYONE A FAIR WAGE FOR THE AMOUNT THEY WORK.

LYNE

OBJECTION! COOK, WHAT YOU REQUEST IS COMPLETE POPPYCOCK. THESE ARE WORKING CLASS MEN, GENTLEMEN. IF THEY ARE PAID IN CUPS AND PLATES, THEN THEY CAN EAT AND DRINK! THIS SYSTEM MAY NOT BE PERFECT MR PRIME MINISTER, BUT IT IS THE BEST SOLUTION WE HAVE TO RESISTING THE SCOURGE OF FREE TRADE!

COOK

MR PRIME MINISTER, ONCE AGAIN MINISTER LYNE HAS FAILED TO REALISE WHAT THE FREE TRADERS STAND FOR. YOU FORCE YOURSELF TO PAY LOWER CLASS FAMILIES WITH WHAT YOU CAN SCROUNGE FROM THE WRECKAGE OF YOUR TRADE MINISTRY. AND AS A RESULT, EVERYBODY SUFFERS. THE LOWER CLASSES CAN BE EASILY EXPLOITED AND THIS IS WHEN THEY WILL BEGIN TO JUDGE US. WE ARE LUCKY MEN. WE HAVE WORKED HARD TO GET TO WHERE WE ARE, AND NOW WE ARE STOPPING PEOPLE FROM BEING ABLE TO DO THE SAME.

LYNE

IS THIS ALL YOU CARE ABOUT COOK? PUBLIC IMAGE? YOU ARE PATHETIC!

<u>HUGHES</u>

LET HIM SPEAK MINISTER LYNE. I WOULD LIKE TO HEAR WHAT COOK
HAS TO SAY ABOUT THIS ISSUE.

<u>COOK</u>

THANK YOU. IF WE ADOPT MY BILL TO REGULATE A FAIR AND DECENT
WAGE FOR ALL THE PEOPLES OF AUSTRALIA TO BE PAID IN CURRENCY,
THEN NOT ONLY WILL THE PEOPLE BE HAPPY THEY CAN HAVE REASON TO
TRUST THE GOVERNMENT. WE MUST ALLOW THE PUBLIC TO BE ABLE TO
SHARE ONE VALUED CURRENCY.

<u>LYNE</u>

THIS IS OUTRAGEOUS! MR PRIME MINISTER, IF YOU ALLOW THIS BILL
RIDDLED WITH FREE TRADER LIES TO PASS THEN WE MUST DIG OUR OWN
GRAVES. I STILL BELIEVE THAT AUSTRALIA MUST REMAIN A STRONG
INDEPENDENT COUNTRY!

<u>DEAKIN</u>

AFTER MUCH CONSIDERATION, I BELIEVE WHAT COOK SAYS IS MAINLY
DUE TO HIS BELIEF IN FREE TRADE. AND MINISTER LYNE THE ISSUES
YOU RAISED WHILE VERY QUESTIONABLE, I FEEL ARE GOOD ISSUES TO
RAISE. WE SHALL PUT IT TO A VOTE.

*(AN EQUAL AMOUNT OF HANDS ON EACH SIDE ARE RAISED. DEAKIN DOES
NOT RAISE HIS.)*

<u>LYNE</u>

LOOKS LIKE I HAVE OUTDONE YOU AGAIN COOK BY THE VOTE OF THE
PRIME MINISTER HIMSELF. BETTER LUCK NEXT TIME.

DEAKIN

NEVERTHELESS, I DECIDE TO HAVE THIS BILL PASSED BECAUSE YOU ARE RIGHT MINISTER LYNE. AUSTRALIA MUST REMAIN A STRONG INDEPENDENT COUNTRY. AND OUR FIRST STEP MUST BE TO PROVIDE A DECENT WAGE FOR A HARD DAY OF WORK. THE PEOPLE OF AUSTRALIA LOOK UP TO US, SO WE MUST GOVERN WITH THEIR INTERESTS AT HEART NOT JUST OUR OWN.

(CHEERING FROM POLITICIANS. LYNE GRIMACES IN DISGUST. COOK CELEBRATES IN TRIUMPH. LYNE STORMS OFFSTAGE DURING THE CHEERING. COOK IS SO CAUGHT UP IN THE MOMENT THAT HE DOESN'T REALISE.)

(EXEUNT)

ACT II

SCENE 4

(THE METHODIST CHURCH OF LITHGOW, NEW SOUTH WALES. COOK IS ATOP A STAND PREACHING TO A CROWD. MARY IS THERE ALSO. LYNE IS IN THE AUDIENCE UNDERCOVER.)

COOK

I WOULD LIKE TO THANK EACH AND EVERY PERSON WHO HAS COME TO LISTEN TODAY. TODAY WE SHALL TAKE A BREAK FROM OUR REGULAR TEACHINGS ABOUT THE LORD, BECAUSE AS CHRISTIANS WE MUST UNITE IN OUR TIMES OF NEED. AS MEN AND WOMEN OF AUSTRALIA, WE SHARE A BOND BEYOND OUR RELIGIOUS BELIEFS.

PERSON 1

WHAT BOND COULD BE MORE IMPORTANT THAN THE ONE WE SHARE WITH THE LORD OUR GOD?

COOK

I CANNOT ARGUE THAT THERE IS A MORE IMPORTANT BOND THAN THE ONE WE SHARE WITH OUR HEAVENLY FATHER. YET IN HIS DIVINE WISDOM, HE GIFTED US WITH A BROTHERHOOD. AND AS A BROTHERHOOD WE HAVE A RESPONSIBILITY TO CARRY OUT THE MESSAGE OF GOD TO THE REST OF THE WORLD.

PERSON 2

YES, BUT HOW SHOULD WE ACCOMPLISH SUCH A FEAT? WE ARE PREACHED SOMETHING SIMILAR BY THE REVEREND EVERY WEEK.

COOK

YES. HOW SHOULD WE CARRY OUT A MESSAGE OF PEACE AND LOVE, AND HOW SHOULD WE LIVE OUR LIVES ACCORDING TO WHAT THE BIBLE SAYS? I WENT INTO POLITICS, BECAUSE I BELIEVE THAT I CAN HELP CREATE A BETTER COUNTRY BY STAYING TRUE TO CHRISTIAN VIRTUES SUCH AS LOVE AND COMPASSION. LIKE MANY OF YOU, I CAME TO THIS COUNTRY TO FIND WORK AND I HAVE TO SAY, I WORKED HARD AND EVENTUALLY, WAS REWARDED. I WAS MADE GENERAL SECRETARY OF THE WESTERN MINERS ASSOCIATION AND FOR THE FIRST TIME IN MY LIFE, I HELD IN MY HAND A GENUINE POSITION OF POWER.

(CALMED WHISPERINGS FROM CROWD)

I FEEL PROUD TO STAND HERE IN THIS CHURCH TODAY AND SAY THAT I HAVE NEVER LOST SIGHT OF MY FELLOW WORKING MAN.

(CROWD CHEERS)

I RESPECT THE MINERS WHO WORKED FOR ME. MY ACTIONS AS GENERAL SECRETARY HAVE HELPED THE INDUSTRY TO BLOSSOM FURTHER THAN WE EVER HOPED IT COULD. AND BY APPLYING CHRISTIAN VALUES TO YOUR LIFE YOU CAN ACHIEVE SUCCESS IN THE SAME WAY.

LYNE

HA!

(LYNE STANDS UP)

WHAT IS THIS MAN PROPOSING? HE IS TRYING TO PLAY GOD! WHY WOULD A MAN OF YOUR POSITION DO THIS?

COOK

WILLIAM? WHAT ON EARTH ARE YOU DOING HERE?

LYNE

ANSWER MY QUESTION YOU DEMON!

COOK

I WOULD NEVER SAY THAT I WAS TRYING TO PLAY GOD.

73

LYNE

I AM AFRAID YOU ARE WRONG, BROTHER COOK. LADIES AND GENTLEMEN, IT IS MY SOLEMN DUTY AS A CONCERNED PATRIOT TO COME HERE AND EXPOSE THIS MAN PREACHING TO YOU AS A FRAUD.

COOK

HOW DARE YOU LYNE!

LYNE

YOU ARE A FRAUD COOK, AND THE WORST THING IS THAT YOU DO NOT EVEN REALISE IT. I CANNOT STAND BY ANY LONGER WHILE YOU FEED THESE PEOPLE LIES.

(LYNE WALKS OVER TO THE STAND)

DO I HAVE THE ATTENTION OF EVERYBODY HERE? GOOD. I HAVE BEEN SITTING AND LISTENING TO THE THINGS HE TELLS YOU HE HAS DONE. AND I MUST SAY, I FIND A LOT OF IT TO BE HILARIOUSLY UNTRUTHFUL.

(MARY WALKS OVER TO LYNE)

MARY

THAT IS ENOUGH WILLIAM. I WILL NOT ALLOW YOU TO DISRESPECT MY HUSBAND LIKE THIS.

LYNE

OH THIS IS RICH. THE LADY WITH THE IRON GLOVE HERSELF. SEE HOW JOSEPH COOK FAILS TO DEFEND HIMSELF PEOPLE! IT IS BECAUSE HE KNOWS HE IS LYING TO YOU.

COOK

NO IT IS BECAUSE LIKE ME, SHE IS NOT AFRAID TO STAND UP TO BULLIES LIKE YOU LYNE.

74

LYNE

THEN DO KINDLY TELL THEM THE TRUTH ABOUT YOUR TIME AS SECRETARY GENERAL. BECAUSE I DOUBT ANY OF THESE PEOPLE KNOW YOU AS WELL AS I DO. LADIES AND GENTLEMEN, I MET JOSEPH COOK MANY YEARS AGO WHEN HE WAS AN INSECURE MAN, WHO HAD BEEN THRUST INTO WHAT HE CALLS POWER, AND WE FORMED A PARTNERSHIP. TOGETHER, WE DOMINATED THE COAL INDUSTRY, DOUBLING THE PRODUCTION OF COAL, WHICH WAS ALREADY BEING MINED IN TONS BY THE MILLIONS. YET WHENEVER IT CAME TO AN IMPORTANT DECISION YOUR SAVIOUR WAS UNSURE OF WHAT TO DO. I HAD TO HELP HIM DO HIS JOB IN ORDER TO ENSURE WE MET CONSUMER DEMANDS.

COOK

I MUST ADMIT, WHEN I STARTED AT THE POSITION OF GENERAL SECRETARY, I WAS A LITTLE OVERWHELMED. BUT I NEVER LOST SIGHT OF WHAT WE WERE DOING.

LYNE

IS THAT SO? THEN PERHAPS YOU NEVER REALISED WHAT WE WERE DOING IN THE FIRST PLACE. YOU WERE NEVER HELPING THE MINERS BENEFIT FOR THEMSELVES. THE ONLY REASON YOU ALLOWED THE MINERS TO PROSPER WAS FOR THE BENEFIT OF THE INDUSTRY AND NOTHING MORE.

(CROWD GASPS)

NOT ONLY THAT, BUT THIS MAN IS NOT EVEN FIT TO BE CALLED A POLITICIAN.

(COOK LOOKS WITH SHOCK AT LYNE)

JOSEPH COOK KNOWS THAT WITHOUT ME, HE WOULD BE NOTHING.

(COOK'S ANGER GROWS. HE CLENCHES HIS FIST.)

COOK

LYNE, STOP.

LYNE

IN FACT, I WOULD GO SO FAR TO SAY THAT WITHOUT ME, YOU WOULD STILL BE AN INSECURE MAN, STRUGGLING TO FIND A STABLE JOB. YOU WOULD NOT BE ABLE TO FEED YOUR FAMILY IF NOT FOR ME.

COOK

HOW DARE YOU LIE ABOUT MY FAMILY IN SUCH A WAY YOU SNAKE! GET OUT! I ORDER YOU TO LEAVE THIS PLACE RIGHT NOW LYNE!

(CROWD BEGINS TO MURMUR. THEY ARE BEGINNING TO DOUBT JOSEPH'S LEADERSHIP.)

MARY

THAT WILL BE ALL FOR NOW. THANK YOU ALL FOR COMING.

(EXIT CROWD. MARY SHAKES JOSEPH BY THE SHOULDERS.)

WHAT IN THE NAME OF GOD WERE YOU THINKING JOSEPH? YOU ARE A POLITICIAN! YOU CANNOT AFFORD TO LOSE YOUR TEMPER LIKE THIS.

COOK

I KNOW BUT I COULD NOT STAND BY WHILE HE INSULTED MY NAME AND MY FAMILY. HE HAS INSULTED EVERYTHING I HOLD DEAR TO MY HEART.

MARY

BUT YOU NEED TO TRY JOSEPH. THE PUBLIC MUST VIEW THE GOVERNMENT AS A POSITIVE FORCE RATHER THAN A NEGATIVE ONE, AND THIS WILL NOT HELP AT ALL.

(LYNE LAUGHS MENACINGLY)

LYNE

YES JOSEPH. LISTEN TO YOUR WIFE, SHE KNOWS BEST. TRUTHFULLY, I NEVER EXPECTED SUCH A VIOLENT TONE FROM A PACIFIST.

COOK

I HAVE NOTHING TO SAY TO YOU LYNE. I HOPE THIS IS A LESSON TO YOU. NEVER INSULT MY FAMILY AGAIN!

LYNE

I SHALL BEAR THAT IN MIND.

(LYNE LAUGHS AGAIN)

BUT THIS HAS TURNED OUT EVEN BETTER THAN I HAD PLANNED.

COOK

WHAT ARE YOU TALKING ABOUT?

LYNE

I HAD A LONG THINK ABOUT WHAT YOU SAID IN PARLIAMENT JOSEPH, AND I STARTED TO SEE MANY OF YOUR POINTS. THAT IS WHY I CAME HERE TODAY. I THOUGHT, WHAT IF I INFLUENCE PUBLIC OPINION OF YOU TO EXPOSE YOU FOR THE FRAUD YOU ARE. BUT I NEVER EXPECTED A BACKLASH LIKE THIS. IT WILL BE BEAUTIFUL.

COOK

GET OUT OF MY SIGHT LYNE! YOU MAY HAVE SULLIED MY NAME TODAY, BUT YOU WILL NEVER SULLY THE FREE TRADERS.

(LYNE LAUGHS MENACINGLY AGAIN)

LYNE

THAT IS WHERE YOU ARE WRONG JOSEPH. YOUR FAT FRIEND REID HAS RESIGNED. HE IS GONE, NOT JUST FROM YOUR PARTY, BUT FROM THIS COUNTRY. HE HAS GONE BACK TO ENGLAND WHERE HE BELONGS, WHICH MAKES YOU THE LEADER OF THE FREE TRADE PARTY BY DEFAULT IN HIS ABSENCE. JUST THINK WHAT THE PUBLIC WILL THINK OF THE FREE TRADERS WHEN THIS NEWS GETS OUT TO THE PUBLIC. THEY WILL DESTROY YOU JOSEPH. YOUR PATHETIC FREE TRADE POLICIES WILL NEVER AGAIN SET FOOT IN THIS COUNTRY.

COOK

WHY? WHY WOULD YOU DO THIS TO ME?

LYNE

BECAUSE WHAT YOU BELIEVE IS WRONG. YOU MUST UNDERSTAND JOSEPH.
I AM TRYING TO SAVE YOU FROM YOURSELF. I SHALL SEE MYSELF OUT.
GOOD LUCK IN THE POLLS.

(EXIT LYNE)

MARY

WHAT HAS HAPPENED TO YOUR FRIEND JOSEPH? YOU AND HE ALWAYS GOT
ALONG SO WELL.

COOK

I KNEW HE WAS A TROUBLED MAN. BUT FOR ALL HIS FAULTS I
BELIEVED THAT HE COULD BE TRUSTED. BUT IT IS TOO LATE. HE IS
TOO FAR GONE NOW.

(EXEUNT)

ACT II

SCENE 5

(ELECTION DAY. THERE IS A CROWD GATHERED OUTSIDE THE PARLIAMENT BUILDING AWAITING THE CANDIDATES TO GIVE THEIR FINAL SPEECH BEFORE THE POLLS OPEN. COOK AND MARY ARE IN THE CROWD WATCHING.)

MARY

YOU DID NOT HAVE TO PULL OUT OF THE RACE FOR PRIME MINISTER JOSEPH. I THINK YOU COULD STILL HAVE WON.

COOK

LYNE SET ME UP MARY. I SHOULD HAVE SEEN THIS COMING. HE IS A MANIPULATIVE MAN AT HEART AND HE HAS USED THAT TO BECOME A BRILLIANT POLITICIAN. I CANNOT HELP BUT ADMIRE LYNE FOR HIS BRILLIANT STRATEGIES, BUT HE HAS ALWAYS HAD A COLD HEART. AFTER THE INCIDENT AT THE CHURCH THE FREE TRADE PARTY HAS BECOME A JOKE.

MARY

YOU ACTED ON IMPULSE JOSEPH. ANYONE WOULD WHEN PROVOKED LIKE THAT.

COOK

BUT IT MEANS SO MUCH MORE TO THE PEOPLE MARY. WE LOST BEFORE THE RACE BEGAN, FROM THE MOMENT I LOST MY TEMPER. I SHOULD HAVE KNOWN BETTER. NOW I AM BERATED AND HARASSED INSIDE AND OUT OF PARLIAMENT BECAUSE OF MY ACTIONS.

PERSON 1

WRETCH!

(COOK BITES HIS LIP IN ANGER THEN SIGHS. FISHER AND DEAKIN ENTER SEPARATELY. FISHER WITH HUGHES AND DEAKIN WITH LYNE.)

FISHER

GOOD DAY LADIES AND GENTLEMEN. IT IS GOOD TO SEE THAT SO MANY OF YOU HAVE TURNED UP TO VOTE TODAY. I ONLY WISH MY OPPONENT WAS AS HAPPY TO SEE HOW MANY OF YOU HAVE TURNED OUT TO VOTE AS I AM.

DEAKIN

FISHER, STOP PUTTING ON THE SHOW FOR THE CROWD. YOUR POLICIES ARE NOT TOUGH ENOUGH TO CREATE A STRONG GOVERNMENT.

FISHER

OH! SO YOU ADMIT YOUR POLICIES ARE TOUGH DEAKIN?

DEAKIN

YOU ARE AN INTELLIGENT MAN FISHER, BUT YOU DO NOT REALISE THAT FOR A GOVERNMENT TO WORK SOMETIMES ONE MUST BE TOUGH.

FISHER

THEN PERHAPS YOU WOULD LIKE TO ELABORATE ON WHY YOU NEED TO BE RE-ELECTED MR PRIME MINISTER.

DEAKIN

I NEED MORE TIME TO FINISH IMPLEMENTING THE POLICIES I STARTED, TO RECTIFY THE PROBLEMS CREATED AFTER YOUR PARTY GAINED OFFICE BY MERE CHANCE.

(CROWD GASPS)

FISHER

I ONLY WISH TO UNDERSTAND WHY YOU DESIRE ANOTHER TERM. ARE YOUR POLICIES REALLY AS TOUGH AS YOU CLAIM? OR ARE YOU TRYING TO HIDE THE FACT YOU ARE A WEAK POLITICIAN STANDING FOR A WEAK PARTY?

DEAKIN

IF WE ARE GOING TO BRING POLITICAL HISTORY INTO THE FRAY NOW, LET ME REMIND EVERYBODY THAT YOUR CANDIDATE CHRIS WATSON WAS NOT ONLY FORCED INTO THE POSITION, BUT SERVED AS PRIME MINISTER FOR ONLY FOUR MONTHS BEFORE RESIGNING. IF WE CAN LEARN ANYTHING FROM THE PAST, IT IS THAT LABOUR ARE NOT FIT FOR GOVERNMENT.

FISHER

YOU APPEAR TO BE STUCK IN THE PAST, OLD MAN. CHRIS WATSON WAS IN MANY EYES OF THE LABOUR PARTY, NOT FIT FOR THE JOB. AFTER ALL, HE WAS KNOWN TO CONSOLIDATE WITH FREE TRADERS.

(CROWD MUTTERS. COOK NARROWS HIS EYES.)

I AM VERY DIFFERENT FROM PAST LEADERS OF THE LABOUR PARTY. I BELIEVE IN A STRONG AUSTRALIA AND I AM THE MAN WHO WILL MAKE IT HAPPEN. WE CANNOT LET OUR COUNTRY BE LEFT IN THE HANDS OF THIS MAN ALFRED DEAKIN BECAUSE HE IS A WEAK LEADER AND AN ADVOCATOR OF FREE TRADE POLICIES.

DEAKIN

FISHER! THIS IS SLANDER! OVER MY TWO TERMS AS PRIME MINISTER, I HAVE CARRIED OUT ALMOST ALL OF MY PROMISES TO THE PEOPLE WITH NO DEVIATION FROM MY POLICIES.

FISHER

NO MATTER. YOU ARE STILL A WEAK LEADER. A LEADER DOES NOT PUT THE PEOPLE HE LEADS SECOND! YOU KNOW MORE THAN A LITTLE BIT ABOUT WEAKNESS DEAKIN. PERHAPS WE SHOULD TALK ABOUT YOUR FIRST TERM.

DEAKIN

THERE IS NO NEED TO BRING THAT UP AGAIN.

FISHER

IF YOU WILL NOT TELL THEM. I WILL.

DEAKIN

GIVE ME MY DIGNITY YOUNG MAN. YOU FORGET YOURSELF.

FISHER

YOU ALL MAY THINK MY OPPONENT HAS TOLD YOU EVERYTHING ABOUT HIS TIME IN OFFICE. HE HAS NOT. MOST POLITICIANS NEVER WILL. HE IS A LIAR WHO NEEDS TO BE PUT IN HIS PLACE.

COOK

DO YOU HAVE ANY PROOF?

FISHER

MY PROOF IS IN HIS ACTIONS COOK. HE WASTED HIS FIRST TERM, FAILING TO PASS ANY LEGISLATION TO IMPROVE THE COUNTRY. THEN HE GAVE UP AND ALLOWED YOUR KIND TO INFECT OUR BELOVED PARLIAMENT. A STRONG LEADER SHOULD NOT LIE TO HIS PEOPLE, OR LET THE INSTITUTION BECOME COMPROMISED BECAUSE OF HIS ACTIONS. YOU ALL KNOW HIS POLICIES, BUT I SAY THAT NOW IS THE TIME FOR NEW POLICIES, A NEW START AND A NEW AUSTRALIA!

(CROWD CHEERS. FISHER RAISES HIS HANDS IN TRIUMPH BEFORE EXITING.)

DEAKIN

YOU CAN VOTE FOR WHOEVER YOU WANT TO. THE LABOUR PARTY CANNOT OFFER YOU ANYTHING NEW AS A GOVERNMENT. I HAVE BEEN YOUR PRIME MINISTER FOR OVER THREE YEARS. I HAVE BEEN THERE FOR YOU IN GOOD TIMES AND BAD, AND I HAVE ALWAYS BEEN HONEST. REMEMBER THIS WHEN YOU GO AND VOTE AT THE POLLS TODAY.

(EXIT DEAKIN AND LYNE. EXIT CROWD.)

HUGHES

MINISTER COOK, SO GOOD TO SEE YOU!

COOK

GOOD TO SEE YOU AS WELL WILLIAM.

HUGHES

WE ARE PAST THE FORMALITIES OF GOVERNMENT NOW COOK. CALL ME BILLY. EVERYBODY ELSE DOES.

COOK

YOUR MAN FISHER APPEARS TO BE AHEAD IN THE POLLS BILLY. YOU MUST BE PROUD.

HUGHES

ACTUALLY, HE IS A NIGHTMARE TO WORK WITH. FISHER IS A LOUDMOUTH AND HE IS GAINING SUPPORT BY THE DAY.

COOK

REALLY?

HUGHES

YES. IF I WERE YOU I WOULD STAY OUT OF HIS WAY FOR NOW. HE IS ALREADY MAD THAT HE HAS LOST MOST OF THE VOTE TO THE PROTECTIONISTS.

COOK

BUT WHY? HE SPOKE WITH SUCH CONFIDENCE EARLIER.

HUGHES

FISHER IS LOSING SUPPORT. MOST OF HIS FOLLOWERS ARE DEFECTING TO THE PROTECTIONISTS AND FROM WHAT I HAVE HEARD THEY ARE STILL UNHAPPY. THEY LIKE NEITHER DEAKIN NOR FISHER.

COOK

WHO ELSE IS THERE THOUGH?

HUGHES

I BELIEVE YOU WOULD HAVE BEEN A VIABLE CANDIDATE HAD YOU NOT
PULLED OUT OF THE RACE COOK. PEOPLE LIKE YOU MORE THAN YOU
THINK.

(COOK IS STUNNED)

IF I WERE YOU, I WOULD NOT STOP TRYING. FISHER WILL PROBABLY
WIN THIS ELECTION, BUT YOU STILL HAVE THE NEXT ONE TO CAMPAIGN
AGAINST HIM.

(THERE IS AN AWKWARD PAUSE)

COOK

WHY ARE YOU TELLING ME ANY OF THIS?

HUGHES

BECAUSE I RESPECT YOU AS A FELLOW POLITICIAN. I WISH FISHER
COULD LEARN HOW TO DO THE SAME.

(EXIT HUGHES)

COOK

MARY, WE NEED TO GO HOME. QUICKLY. I HAVE AN IDEA.

(EXEUNT)

SCENE 6

(THE COOK HOUSEHOLD, 1908. THE CHILDREN ARE GATHERED AROUND A CHESS BOARD PLAYING CHESS. JOSEPH IS ON THE OTHER SIDE OF THE STAGE SITTING IN HIS STUDY LOOKING PENSIVELY INTO THE DISTANCE, IN BETWEEN.)

COOK

CURSE THIS INFERNAL PAPERWORK. WILL IT NEVER END?

(ENTER MARY CARRYING A TRAY WITH TEA ON IT. SHE POURS HIM A CUP.)

MARY

THE TEA IS READY JOSEPH. I WOULD WAIT A WHILE THOUGH AND LEAVE IT TO COOL. IT IS VERY HOT.

COOK

THANK YOU MARY. LEAVE IT ON THE SIDE.

(MARY KNEELS DOWN)

MARY

JOSEPH IF THERE IS SOMETHING WRONG YOU NEED TO TELL ME. YOU HAVE BEEN VERY DISTANT LATELY.

COOK

I AM FINE MARY. THERE IS NOTHING TO WORRY ABOUT.

MARY

BUT THIS IS NOT YOU. DO NOT SHUT ME OUT, LET ME IN SO I CAN HELP. I KNOW THERE IS SOMETHING TROUBLING YOU JOSEPH. JUST TELL ME WHAT IT IS, PLEASE.

CHILD 2

CHECK.

COOK

MARY, ALL I FOUGHT FOR IS CRUMBLING. THE PEOPLE ARE NO LONGER INTERESTED IN THE IDEA OF A GOVERNMENT FOUNDED UPON THE PRINCIPLES OF FREE TRADE.

MARY

TRUST ME JOSEPH, BILLY HUGHES THINKS VERY HIGHLY OF YOU. IS THAT NOT ENOUGH REASON TO TRY?

COOK

MARY MY LOVE, HE IS ONLY BEING POLITE. HE RESPECTS ME AS A POLITICIAN BUT OUR RELATIONSHIP IS NOTHING MORE THAN THAT. WE ARE ON OPPOSITE SIDES OF A PARLIAMENT WHICH DOES NOT WISH TO BACK ME.

CHILD 1

CHECK.

MARY

IF YOU ARE SO EAGER TO GIVE UP, THEN I SUPPOSE YOU WILL NOT WANT TO READ THIS.

(MARY SHOWS JOSEPH A LETTER)

COOK

WHAT IS THIS?

MARY

HE HAS WRITTEN TO YOU. TO US. AND HE SAYS THAT HE WANTS TO
MEET WITH YOU, WHEN YOU HAVE THE TIME OF COURSE. HE MAY WORK
FOR LABOUR, BUT HE SEES POTENTIAL IN YOU.

CHILD 2

CHECK.

COOK

YOU ARE RIGHT MARY, I WILL NEVER ACHIEVE ANYTHING SITTING HERE
FEELING SORRY FOR MYSELF. I NEED TO WORK ON MY CAMPAIGN FOR
THE NEXT ELECTION. BUT I DO NOT KNOW WHERE TO START,
ESPECIALLY CONCERNING THE PUBLIC FRONT.

MARY

YES THAT IS A PROBLEM. THE PUBLIC WILL NOT COME AROUND EASILY,
DESPITE WHAT HUGHES SAYS.

(THERE IS A KNOCK AT THE DOOR)

CHILD 1

CHECK.

MARY

I WONDER WHO THAT COULD BE AT THIS HOUR?

COOK

WHOEVER IT IS, I DO NOT WANT TO TALK TO THEM. I HAVE ENOUGH
PROBLEMS TO DEAL WITH AT THE MOMENT.

MARY

(TO CHILDREN)

COULD YOU ANSWER THE DOOR?

CHILD 1

BUT I AM WINNING.

MARY

ANSWER THE DOOR.

CHILD 1

(*SIGHS*)

YES MOTHER.

(*OPENS THE DOOR TO FIND DEAKIN AND A SCOWLING LYNE STANDING IN THE DOORWAY*)

HELLO? CAN I HELP YOU?

DEAKIN

GOOD EVENING YOUNG MASTER COOK. WE WISH TO SPEAK WITH YOUR FATHER. CAN YOU FETCH HIM FOR US?

(*CHILD GOES AND FETCHES COOK AND BRINGS HIM TO THE DOOR*)

COOK

DEAKIN? WHAT ARE YOU DOING HERE?

DEAKIN

WE NEED TO SPEAK WITH YOU JOSEPH. IT IS AN URGENT MATTER.

COOK

OF COURSE. COME IN.

(*DEAKIN AND LYNE ENTER COOK'S HOME. AS LYNE PASSES COOK HE GIVES COOK AN EVIL STARE.*)

WHAT CAN I DO FOR YOU GENTLEMEN?

LYNE

FOR THE RECORD I WOULD LIKE TO SAY THAT I DO NOT WANT TO BE
HERE.

DEAKIN

BUT YOU CAME BECAUSE IT IS THE ONLY WAY TO ENSURE THE SURVIVAL
OF OUR PARTY.

COOK

WHAT ARE YOU TALKING ABOUT? THE PROTECTIONISTS HAVE BEEN DOING
RATHER WELL RECENTLY IN PARLIAMENT.

DEAKIN

THAT USED TO BE THE CASE, BUT SADLY NOT ANYMORE. THE LABOUR
PARTY HAS BECOME TOO POWERFUL FOR US TO DEFEAT IN THE POLLS BY
OURSELVES. FISHER PROPOSES POLICIES THAT WILL END UP
BANKRUPTING THE ECONOMY IF HE IS ALLOWED TO SERVE ANOTHER
TERM. THAT IS WHY WE NEED YOUR HELP AND YOUR SKILLS AS A
SPEAKER TO DEFEAT HIM IN THE POLLS.

COOK

I MUST ADMIT, I HAVE HAD MY DOUBTS ABOUT FISHER RECENTLY.

DEAKIN

YOU ARE ONE OF THE MOST DEDICATED MEMBERS I HAVE SEEN ACT IN
PARLIAMENT, AND WE WOULD BE HONOURED TO RECEIVE YOUR HELP IN
ANY WAY WE CAN.

COOK

I WOULD BE MORE THAN HAPPY TO HELP IF YOU THINK A PARTNERSHIP
IS EVEN POSSIBLE. WE WOULD HAVE TO NEGOTIATE OUR POLICIES IF
WE ARE TO WORK TOGETHER.

DEAKIN

OF COURSE MY FRIEND.

COOK

VERY WELL. THOUGH TO HAVE A DEAL, WE MUST FUSE OUR PARTIES
TOGETHER TO FORM ONE WHICH EMBODIES THE FINEST PRINCIPLES OF
BOTH. BUT ARE WE GOING TO BE POPULAR ENOUGH TO DEFEAT FISHER
IN THE POLLS?

DEAKIN

WE CAN DO GREAT THINGS IF WE WORK TOGETHER. FISHER HAS FOUND
OUT THAT BEING PRIME MINISTER IS NOT SO EASY AS IT SOUNDS, AND
THE PEOPLE KNOW IT TOO. HE IS LOSING THE PUBLIC, SO THIS IS
OUR BEST CHANCE TO BEAT HIM AT HIS OWN GAME.

LYNE

HE IS A SMART MAN THOUGH, AND HE WILL NOT GO DOWN EASILY.

DEAKIN

WHAT SAY YOU JOSEPH?

COOK

I SAY WE MAKE PLANS GENTLEMEN. IF WE ARE TO GOVERN AUSTRALIA
PROPERLY, WE NEED TO STRATEGIZE.

(EXEUNT)

INTERVAL

ACT II

ACT II

SCENE 7

(THE AUSTRALIAN PARLIAMENT, 1909. COOK AND LYNE ARE WORKING HARD AT THE DESK OF THE NEWLY ELECTED PRIME MINISTER, ALFRED DEAKIN.)

COOK

WILLIAM MY FRIEND, I STILL WONDER HOW WE EVER WON THE ELECTION.

LYNE

FISHER IS AN INTELLIGENT MAN, BUT A WEAK LEADER, AND NOW HE HAS PAID THE PRICE FOR IT. THE PEOPLE SEE THROUGH HIM.

COOK

WE HAVE MORE IMPORTANT THINGS TO WORRY ABOUT THAN FISHER NOW. WE HAVE JOINED TOGETHER TO RUN THE COUNTRY AND WE HAVE A RESPONSIBILITY TO DO SO WITH RESPECT FOR THE PEOPLE.

LYNE

IF YOU SAY SO COOK, BUT REMEMBER WHAT WE AGREED IN FORMING THIS COALITION. THE PROSPERITY OF AUSTRALIA MUST COME FIRST.

(ENTER DEAKIN)

DEAKIN

INDEED IT MUST GENTLEMEN. BUT I FIND THAT WE MUST REACH OUT TO THE PEOPLE IF AUSTRALIA IS TO PROSPER. COOK, DO YOU HAVE THE NAVAL LEGISLATION?

COOK

YES MR PRIME MINISTER. MAY I ASK WHAT THIS IS ABOUT?

DEAKIN

AS YOU KNOW THE AUSTRALIAN NAVY IS QUITE SPARSE, SO I HAVE
BEEN LOOKING INTO THE NAVAL DEFENCES OF OTHER COUNTRIES FOR
INSPIRATION. THE JAPANESE HAVE A VERY HIGH STANDARD BECAUSE
THEY ARE AN ISLAND NATION. I BELIEVE WE MUST FOLLOW SUIT IF WE
ARE TO GROW AS A COUNTRY. JOSEPH, I WOULD LIKE YOU TO TAKE
RESPONSIBILITY FOR THE DEVELOPMENT OF SUCH A TASKFORCE.

COOK

OF COURSE ALFRED. BUT WHY WOULD WE NEED A NAVY NOW?

DEAKIN

BECAUSE YOU WERE RIGHT JOSEPH. YOU WERE RIGHT ABOUT REACHING
OUT TO OUR ALLIES FOR PROSPERITY. I HAVE ALSO HEARD FROM OUR
REPRESENTATIVE, EDMUND BARTON BACK IN ENGLAND. HE TELLS OF
GREAT FORCES ALIGNING TOGETHER, MILITARIES FROM ACROSS EUROPE
FUSING TO CREATE STRENGTH IN UNITY.

COOK

AND YOU BELIEVE WE SHOULD DO THE SAME?

DEAKIN

I DO. IF CONFLICT WERE TO ARISE, AUSTRALIA WOULD NOT BE READY
TO INTERVENE. WE WOULD BE PULLED INTO A FIGHT WE ARE NOT READY
FOR. I BELIEVE IF WE WORK TOGETHER WE CAN MAKE AUSTRALIA A
REAL PEACEKEEPING FORCE FOR GOOD.

COOK

IF WE ARE TO USE THIS NAVY TO PREVENT WARS INSTEAD OF CAUSING
THEM, THEN I SHALL GIVE IT MY FULL ATTENTION.

DEAKIN

FANTASTIC.

(JOSEPH WALKS OFF TO THE SIDE TO BEGIN HIS WORK. DEAKIN TURNS
TO LYNE.)

LYNE, CAN YOU LOOK INTO SOURCING MATERIALS AND MEN WE CAN USE
TO BUILD THE SHIPS?

LYNE

I CAN. AND MIGHT I SAY MR PRIME MINISTER, THIS PROJECT SOUNDS
AS IF IT WILL PROVIDE MANY JOBS FOR AUSTRALIANS.

DEAKIN

IT SHALL WILLIAM, IT SHALL. MIGHT I SUGGEST THAT FOR RAW
MATERIALS YOU LOOK AT POSSIBLE TRADING OPTIONS WITH CLOSE
COLONIAL TERRITORIES. NEW ZEALAND WOULD BE A GOOD PLACE TO
START.

LYNE

CAN WE NOT RELY ON OUR OWN MATERIALS? IF WE WANT TO BUILD A
FLEET FOR OUR COUNTRY THEN IT SHOULD BE PURE.

(COOK COMES BACK OVER)

DEAKIN

I HAVE TOLD YOU THIS TIME AND TIME AGAIN WILLIAM, POLITICS
SHOULD NOT BE ABOUT PURITY. MANY OF OUR PRINCIPLES WERE
FOUNDED ON IDEOLOGIES THAT DREW TOO HEAVILY FROM PURITY AND IT
LEAD US TO RUIN.

LYNE

YOU FORGET YOURSELF SIR. ARE YOU NOT THE LEADER OF THIS
COUNTRY? DO YOU NOT WANT TO BUILD A NAVY FOR THE AUSTRALIAN
PEOPLE?

DEAKIN

YOU MUST UNDERSTAND THAT WE NEED ALL THE HELP WE CAN TAKE IF
WE ARE TO SUCCEED IN BUILDING SUCH A FLEET. WE CANNOT BE SEEN
AS WEAK, THAT IS WHY WE NEED ALLIES.

LYNE

JUDAS!!! THE ONLY WEAK ONE HERE IS YOU DEAKIN! YOU HAVE LED
THE PROTECTIONISTS INTO RUIN THROUGH THE FAULT OF YOUR OWN
STUPID PRACTICES! I HAVE FOLLOWED YOU EVERY STEP OF THE WAY
BECAUSE I BELIEVE IN PROTECTIONISM, BUT NOW I KNOW THE TRUTH!
YOU CARE NOT FOR THE VALUES OF YOUR OWN PARTY, YOU ONLY CARE
ABOUT BEING IN CONTROL. YOU LUST AFTER POWER, AND NOW YOU HAVE
PAID THE PRICE! YOU ARE NO LONGER A PROTECTIONIST! YOU HAVE
BETRAYED EVERYTHING WE STOOD FOR! YOU HAVE SOLD YOUR SOUL TO
THE FREE TRADERS WITH YOUR FUSION PRINCIPLES! I WILL NOT BE A
PART OF IT! I REFUSE!

COOK

WILLIAM, CALM DOWN. IF WE BEGIN TO ARGUE THEN WE WILL ACHIEVE
NOTHING.

LYNE

ACHIEVE NOTHING? WE ALREADY HAVE! TO THINK, I ONCE HAD ALL THE
RESPECT IN THE WORLD FOR YOU COOK. NOW I SEE THAT YOU ARE
NOTHING BUT A PARASITE, WHO LIVES OFF THE WEALTH OF OTHERS TO
SURVIVE. YOU WILL BOTH BE A DETRIMENT TO AUSTRALIA AND I WILL
NO LONGER BE BRANDED AS A WEAK MAN BECAUSE OF YOUR INFECTIOUS
FREE TRADE POLICIES. I WILL HAVE NO PART IN YOUR INEVITABLE
FAILURE! GENTLEMEN, GOODBYE!

(EXIT LYNE)

COOK

WHAT DO WE DO NOW ALFRED? AS A PARTY WE CANNOT AFFORD TO
DIVIDE.

94

DEAKIN

WE MUST CARRY ON. WILLIAM NEVER SEEMED TO AGREE WITH ME ABOUT THE FUSION. THERE ARE TROUBLING TIMES AHEAD JOSEPH. OUR GOVERNMENT MUST BE STRONG WITHOUT HIM OR PERISH.

(EXEUNT)

ACT II

SCENE 8

(FISHER IS ALONE ONSTAGE. HE IS PACING AND LOOKING AROUND THE AUDIENCE FOR SOMETHING. HE LOOKS LIKE HE'S GETTING MORE IMPATIENT BY THE MINUTE.)

FISHER

WHERE IS HE? THIS MEETING WAS HIS IDEA. IF HE IS NOT HERE SOON THEN THE ARRANGEMENT WILL BE OFF.

(ENTER LYNE SPEAKING HIS LINES)

LYNE

NOW, NOW FISHER, WE CANNOT HAVE THAT CAN WE? TO HAVE YOU ABANDONING YOUR POST WOULD BE VERY.

(BREATHES)

DISLOYAL.

FISHER

YOU ARE LATE LYNE. THIS HAS NOTHING TO DO WITH LOYALTY, UNLESS YOU ARE PLEDGING IT TO ME. IS THIS WHY YOU ARRANGED THIS LITTLE MEETING BETWEEN US?

LYNE

NOT EXACTLY. I CAME TO WARN YOU ANDREW. AUSTRALIA IS DYING. THE FUSION GOVERNMENT IS RUNNING THE COUNTRY INTO THE GROUND WITH THEIR LIBERAL POLICIES AND AGENDAS.

FISHER

AND YOU HAVE COME TO ME FOR HELP?

LYNE

I HAVE COME TO PROPOSE AN ALLIANCE, BECAUSE SOMETHING MUST BE
DONE ABOUT THE FREE TRADE IDEOLOGIES THEY ARE RUINING OUR
COUNTRY WITH.

FISHER

VERY WELL. I SHALL CONSIDER YOUR PROPOSAL. BUT I WILL NEED
SOMETHING TO GUARANTEE YOUR ALLEGIANCE. THINK OF IT AS A TOKEN
OF YOUR FAITH.

LYNE

I CAN GIVE YOU MY WORD.

FISHER

THAT IS NOT ENOUGH.

LYNE

AND I CAN TELL YOU EVERYTHING YOU NEED TO KNOW ABOUT THE
COMMONWEALTH LIBERAL PARTY. I CAN TELL YOU THEIR STRENGTHS AND
THEIR WEAKNESSES. DEAKIN WILL NOT BE ABLE TO STOP YOU.

FISHER

MUCH BETTER. I PRIZE KNOWLEDGE VERY HIGHLY WHEN IT COMES TO
POLITICS.

LYNE

SO, WE ARE IN AGREEMENT THEN?

FISHER

YES. UNDER MY IRON FIST, AUSTRALIA WILL BE A STRONG COUNTRY
AGAIN. THE DAYS OF BEING A LAUGHING STOCK WILL BE OVER
WILLIAM. I CAN ASSURE YOU THAT. COME. A BRIGHT FUTURE AWAITS
FOR ALL OF US.

<u>LYNE</u>

WITH MY CUNNING PLAN AND YOUR INFLUENCE IN PARLIAMENT, WE
SHALL LEAD AUSTRALIA TO GREATNESS. NOW HERE IS WHAT I WANT YOU
TO DO...

(EXEUNT TOGETHER DISCUSSING THE PLAN)

ACT II

SCENE 9

(FISHER AND DEAKIN ARE ONSTAGE CAMPAIGNING FOR THE POSITION OF PRIME MINISTER AGAIN IN FRONT OF A CROWD. LYNE AND COOK ARE ONSTAGE WITH THEIR RESPECTIVE CANDIDATES.)

FISHER

MY FRIENDS, AUSTRALIA NEEDS TO BECOME A BEACON OF GLORY FOR THE PEOPLE AGAIN. THE COMMONWEALTH LIBERAL PARTY MAY HAVE CONVINCED YOU THAT THEY ARE A PARTY THAT WORKS FOR THE GREATER GOOD OF THE PEOPLE OF AUSTRALIA, BUT MAKE NO MISTAKE! THESE POLICIES ARE FREE TRADE LIES!

DEAKIN

YOU ARE THE LIAR FISHER. THE COMMONWEALTH LIBERAL PARTY HAS BEEN DOING VERY GOOD WORK FOR THE BENEFIT OF THE NATION, AND WILL CONTINUE TO DO SO AFTER I AM RE-ELECTED.

FISHER

MORE AND MORE LIES. WHEN WILL YOU STOP DECEIVING THE GOOD PEOPLE OF AUSTRALIA DEAKIN?

DEAKIN

I AM DOING NOTHING OF THE SORT YOU SLANDEROUS VIPER!

FISHER

UNLIKE MR DEAKIN, I CARE ABOUT THE FUTURE OF THIS COUNTRY. AND THAT IS WHY TODAY, I PLEDGE TO STRENGTHEN THE AUSTRALIAN NAVY, REDUCE TAXES AND CREATE JOBS FOR ALL.

(CHEERING FROM CROWD. EXIT FISHER. COOK PULLS LYNE ASIDE.)

COOK

WHAT HAVE YOU DONE?

LYNE

WHAT DO YOU MEAN, WHAT HAVE I DONE?

COOK

DO NOT DENY YOUR INVOLVEMENT. I KNOW YOU HAVE BEEN HELPING FISHER. HOW ELSE COULD HE KNOW INSIDE INFORMATION ABOUT THE COMMONWEALTH LIBERAL PARTY? HOW COULD YOU DO THIS TO YOUR COLLEAGUES?

LYNE

THE MOMENT DEAKIN CAME TO YOU FOR HELP IT STOPPED BEING MY PARTY. DEAKIN BETRAYED US AND AS A RESULT I AM NOW THE SOLE SURVIVOR OF TRUE PROTECTIONISM.

COOK

YOU BOTH NEEDED HELP. WITHOUT ME THE PROTECTIONISTS AND THE FREE TRADERS WOULD NOT EXIST. DEAKIN IS MORE OF A SURVIVOR THAN YOU WILL EVER BE. I THOUGHT THAT YOU COULD BE GRATEFUL FOR WHAT WE WERE ABLE TO ACCOMPLISH TOGETHER BUT YOU ARE SO FIXATED ON THIS LIE THAT DEAKIN IS A BAD MAN.

LYNE

HE IS! THAT JUDAS HAS LED THE PROTECTIONISTS TO RUIN AND (*COUGHS*) HE WILL LEAVE YOU TO ROT ON THE CROSS LIKE YOUR SAVIOUR, JUST AS HE DID TO TRUE PROTECTIONIST IDEALS!

(*EXIT LYNE*)

COOK

WILLIAM! WILLIAM COME BACK!

(*DEAKIN WALKS OVER TO COOK*)

DEAKIN

WHAT WAS THAT ABOUT JOSEPH?

COOK

IT WAS NOTHING. BUT I FEAR I CANNOT HELP LYNE NOW. HIS DELUSIONS HAVE BECOME MUCH WORSE THAN I FEAR.

DEAKIN

I AM SORRY TO HEAR THAT YOU HAVE LOST YOUR FRIEND JOSEPH, BUT I NEED TO TALK TO YOU ABOUT THE FUTURE OF THE PARTY.

(COOK LOOKS TOWARDS DEAKIN)

(SIGHS)

I AM GETTING TOO OLD FOR POLITICS JOSEPH. IT IS A GAME FOR YOUNGER MEN, AND AS THE DAYS GO BY I AM FINDING IT HARDER TO COMPOSE MYSELF AS A DEBATER.

COOK

YOU ARE RETIRING?

DEAKIN

NOT ENTIRELY FROM POLITICS, BUT I HAVE REALISED I NEED TO STEP BACK ONTO THE BENCH JOSEPH. I CANNOT DO THIS ANYMORE. SO FROM THIS MOMENT ON, I WANT YOU TO TAKE CHARGE OF THE COMMONWEALTH LIBERAL PARTY. YOU ARE POPULAR WITH THE PEOPLE AND I WANT YOU TO PROMISE ME SOMETHING MY FRIEND.

COOK

OF COURSE ALFRED.

DEAKIN

NEVER GIVE IN TO FISHER AND HIS LIES. NEVER STOP TRYING TO CREATE AN AUSTRALIA THAT CAN BE GOOD AND TRUE. YOU NEED TO FINISH WHAT WE STARTED, TO NOT LET THIS ALL BE IN VAIN.

COOK

I GIVE YOU MY WORD ALFRED. I WILL NEVER STOP TRYING TO CREATE
A BETTER AUSTRALIA FOR ALL.

DEAKIN

THANK YOU JOSEPH. YOU ARE THE KIND OF MAN THIS COUNTRY
DESERVES. MAKE IT HAPPEN.

(EXEUNT)

ACT II

SCENE 10

(LYNE IS ONSTAGE. ENTER FISHER.)

FISHER

WHAT DO YOU WANT LYNE, I AM A VERY BUSY MAN.

LYNE

I NEED TO TALK TO YOU ABOUT THE ISSUE OF JOSEPH COOK.

FISHER

I DO NOT HAVE TIME FOR THIS LYNE. JOSEPH COOK IS IRRELEVANT, WE DID WHAT WE SET OUT TO DO. I AM NOW PRIME MINISTER AND THE COUNTRY TRUSTS ME. THEY KNOW EVERYTHING I DO IS FOR THEIR BENEFIT.

LYNE

NOTHING COULD BE FURTHER FROM THE TRUTH FISHER. COOK AND HIS NEW CAMPAIGN IS BEGINNING TO GAIN MOMENTUM, AND HIS POPULARITY IS SOARING.

FISHER

EVEN IF HIS POPULARITY IS GROWING HE CANNOT DEFEAT ME IN THE POLLS.

LYNE

YOU DO NOT KNOW COOK LIKE I DO. HE IS SMARTER THAN YOU THINK AND WILL GO TO ANY LENGTHS TO SUCCEED. THAT MAKES HIM A DANGEROUS OPPONENT.

103

FISHER

IF COOK IS AS DANGEROUS AS YOU SAY, WHY DID YOU NOT WARN ME
EARLIER?

LYNE

I NEVER THOUGHT HE WOULD GAIN MOMENTUM AGAIN. BUT IN THIS
COUNTRY IT IS CLEAR ANYTHING CAN HAPPEN. WE HAVE HAD SO MANY
PRIME MINISTERS ELECTED IN SUCH A SHORT SPACE OF TIME, I FEAR
IT COULD HAPPEN AGAIN.

FISHER

I AM CONCERNED FOR YOU LYNE. I THINK YOU MAY BE STARTING TO
LOSE YOUR GRIP ON WHAT WE ARE DOING HERE. YOU SEEM TO HAVE AN
UNHEALTHY OBSESSION WITH JOSEPH COOK.

LYNE

I DO NOT CARE! I WILL NOT REST UNTIL THE FREE TRADERS ARE NO
MORE.

(*GRIMACES IN PAIN*)

FISHER

LYNE, WHAT IS WRONG?

LYNE

IT IS ONLY MY GOUT. DO NOT WORRY ABOUT ME. WORRY ABOUT COOK.

FISHER

BUT HOW WILL I DEFEAT HIM IF HE IS AS DANGEROUS AS YOU SAY?

LYNE

I WILL NOT LIE TO YOU FISHER. YOU WILL NOT BE ABLE TO BEAT
COOK IN THE POLLS.

FISHER

WHAT!? YOU TELL ME THIS NOW!?

LYNE

BUT IF YOU GAIN A MAJORITY IN THE SENATE COOK WILL NOT BE ABLE TO PASS ANY BILLS. IF COOK DOES BEAT YOU, YOU WILL REMAIN IN POWER AS LONG AS YOU OWN THE SENATE MAJORITY.

FISHER

OF COURSE! IF I HOLD THE SENATE THEN IT DOES NOT MATTER WHO IS IN CHARGE OF THE COUNTRY. WE HAVE WORK TO DO LYNE. START WRITING LETTERS TO ALL SENATE OFFICIALS. WHEN THE ELECTION COMES, COOK WILL NOT STAND A CHANCE. THIS IS HIS LAST GOOD NIGHT MY FRIEND. THANK YOU.

(EXEUNT FISHER LAUGHING AND LYNE LIMPING)

ACT II

SCENE 11

(1913. CROWD IS ONSTAGE. ENTER COOK AND MARY. COOK STEPS UP TO THE PODIUM WITH MARY BESIDE HIM.)

COOK

WELCOME LADIES AND GENTLEMEN TO THE FINAL ELECTION DEBATE OF 1913. I WOULD LIKE TO BEGIN BY SAYING, I HOPE ANY VIEWS OF ME THAT YOU HAVE HAD IN THE PAST CAN BE WIPED CLEAN HERE. MY WISH IS FOR US ALL TO START ANEW, FOR THE GOOD OF THE PEOPLE OF AUSTRALIA.

(ENTER FISHER, MARCHING OVER TO THE PODIUM.)

FISHER

JOSEPH, PLEASE. DO NOT LIE TO THESE GOOD PEOPLE.

COOK

I AM NO LIAR FISHER. I BELIEVE YOU KNOW THIS.

FISHER

IT IS WORSE THAN I THOUGHT. JOSEPH COOK, LORD AND SAVIOUR OF THE PEOPLE OF AUSTRALIA HAS MANAGED TO CONVINCE HIMSELF THAT HE IS A GOOD MAN. HEED THESE WORDS CITIZENS, JOSEPH COOK IS LYING TO YOU.

COOK

DELUSIONAL!

FISHER

LET ME FINISH, MR COOK. MAKE NO MISTAKE PEOPLE, HE DOES NOT CARE ABOUT YOU. THE POLICIES THIS MAN WILL ENACT WILL SET THIS COUNTRY BACK, NOT BRING PROGRESS.

COOK

YOU DO NOT KNOW THE FULL EXTENT OF MY POLICIES FISHER.

FISHER

PERHAPS NOT, BUT I DO KNOW THAT THESE POLICIES ARE NOT GOOD FOR AUSTRALIA. I HAVE ALWAYS PUT THE NEEDS OF THE COUNTRY FIRST AND YOU SEEK TO CHANGE THIS.

(COOK IGNORES FISHER)

COOK

LADIES, GENTLEMEN. CHILDREN OF AUSTRALIA. WE STAND AT THE FOREFRONT OF A NATION WISHING TO BE REBORN. AND I PROMISE YOU I CAN AND WILL BRING CHANGE FOR THE BENEFIT OF EVERY AUSTRALIAN CITIZEN.

FISHER

BENEFITS? WHAT BENEFITS? YOU HAVE FAILED TO BRING PROGRESS TO AUSTRALIA EVERY TIME YOU HAVE TRIED.

(COOK CONTINUES TO IGNORE FISHER)

COOK

LET ME FINISH. MY FRIENDS, ANDREW FISHER IS A MAN WHO DESPERATELY WANTS TO CLING ONTO POWER ANY WAY HE CAN.

FISHER

(GASPS)

YOU LIAR!

COOK

DO YOU REALLY WANT SOMEONE THAT DESPERATE GOVERNING YOUR COUNTRY? I CERTAINLY WOULD NOT, BECAUSE HE WOULD MAKE RASH DECISIONS BASED ON FEAR OF LOSING HIS POWER.

FISHER

I NEVER MAKE RASH DECISIONS COOK. COOK?

COOK

SO WHEN YOU VOTE FOR THE NEXT PRIME MINISTER, I IMPLORE YOU TO VOTE FOR SOMEONE WHO WILL BE A STRONG AND EFFICIENT LEADER. VOTE FOR JOSEPH COOK!

(CROWD CHEERS AND EXITS)

MARY

JOSEPH THAT WAS AMAZING! I NEVER THOUGHT I WOULD SEE A SPEECH AS PASSIONATE AS THAT IN ALL MY LIFE.

COOK

THANK YOU MARY, BUT I HAVE NOT WON YET. THE REST IS UP TO THE PEOPLE.

FISHER

YES COOK, YOU HAVE NOT WON YET. FOR YOUR VICTORY TO BE COMPLETE YOU MUST CONSIDER ALL OF THE VOTING POPULATION, NOT JUST THE EASILY LED SHEEP YOU HAVE SO PATHETICALLY WON OVER.

MARY

I THINK YOU ARE JEALOUS FISHER. AFTER ALL, YOUR DEBATING SKILLS COULD USE SOME WORK.

COOK

NOW, NOW MARY, THERE IS NO NEED FOR THIS. WE MUST FOCUS ON THE ELECTION.

FISHER

WATCH YOUR BACK COOK. I SWEAR YOU WILL NOT COME OUT OF THIS WITH WHAT YOU WANT.

(EXIT FISHER)

MARY

WHAT WAS THAT ABOUT?

COOK

I DO NOT KNOW MARY. FISHER CONTINUES TO CONFUSE ME. SHALL WE?

(EXEUNT TOGETHER)

ACT II

SCENE 12

(ENTER COOK, MARY, FISHER, HUGHES AND OFFICIAL. THEY APPROACH A TABLE WITH A BOX FULL OF VOTES. THE OFFICIAL OPENS IT AND BEGINS COUNTING THEM.)

COOK

MAY THE BEST MAN WIN FISHER. GOOD LUCK.

FISHER

I MUST ADMIT COOK, YOU ARE A CUNNING ADVERSARY AND A VERY SKILLED LINGUIST, BUT I AM CONFIDENT THAT THOSE WHO WANT AUSTRALIA TO REMAIN A POWERFUL NATION WILL REMAIN LOYAL TO ME.

MARY

I DOUBT THAT. I RECKON THE PEOPLE WILL SEE THAT MY HUSBAND IS A GREAT EXAMPLE FOR AUSTRALIA TO FOLLOW. I CANNOT SAY THE SAME ABOUT YOU.

COOK

NOW, NOW MARY. LET US BE CIVIL.

FISHER

INDEED. WE SHALL ALL SEE WHO IS LAUGHING AT THE END OF THIS ELECTION. HAVE YOU FINISHED COUNTING YET?

OFFICIAL

BE PATIENT FISHER, I AM ONLY DOING MY DUTY. AND PLEASE DO NOT INTERRUPT ME AGAIN. I DO NOT WANT TO MISCOUNT THE VOTES.

FISHER

VERY WELL. YOU HAVE MADE YOUR POINT.

(FISHER BACKS AWAY FROM THE OFFICIAL. COOK LEANS OVER TOWARDS MARY.)

COOK

I HAVE A GOOD FEELING ABOUT THIS ELECTION MARY.

MARY

I AM NOT SO SURE JOSEPH. I THINK FISHER IS UP TO SOMETHING.

COOK

HE IS A SLY, INTELLIGENT POLITICIAN MARY. NEARLY ALL OF THEM ARE UP TO SOMETHING.

MARY

NO, THIS IS DIFFERENT. DID YOU NOTICE THE WAY HE WAS SPEAKING TO YOU? HE SEEMS VERY CONFIDENT FOR A MAN WHO HAS BEEN BEATEN IN DEBATE.

COOK

I NOTICED THAT AS WELL. I ASSUME HE IS OVERWHELMED BY MY SPEECH.

MARY

PERHAPS NOW IS NOT THE TIME TO THINK ABOUT YOURSELF JOSEPH. SOMETHING DOES NOT FEEL RIGHT AND IT IS MAKING ME FEEL UNEASY.

COOK

NOW YOU MENTION IT, HE HAS BEEN TALKING TO LYNE A LOT RECENTLY. I HOPE HE HAS NOT BEEN INFLUENCED TOO MUCH BY HIS RADICAL IDEOLOGIES.

OFFICIAL

MAY I HAVE YOUR ATTENTION PLEASE. THE VOTES HAVE BEEN TALLIED AND WE HAVE COME TO A RESULT. THIS ELECTION HAS BEEN THE CLOSEST EVER FOR THE AUSTRALIAN PEOPLE, BUT BY A SCORE OF ONE VOTE JOSEPH COOK IS HEREBY ELECTED AS THE PRIME MINISTER OF AUSTRALIA.

COOK

THANKS BE TO GOD! I CAN BARELY BELIEVE IT. MY HARD WORK HAS FINALLY PAID OFF.

MARY

BELIEVE IT JOSEPH, YOU HAVE WORKED LONG AND HARD TO GET HERE, AND NOW YOU ARE PRIME MINISTER. YOU HAVE COME A LONG WAY FROM THE LITTLE BOY WHO USED TO WORK IN THE MINES.

COOK

I AM NOTHING BUT GRATEFUL TO THE PEOPLE OF AUSTRALIA FOR GIVING ME THIS OPPORTUNITY. I CAN FINALLY START TO MAKE REAL CHANGES IN GOVERNMENT.

HUGHES

CONGRATULATIONS ON YOUR VICTORY JOSEPH. IT WAS VERY WELL DESERVED.

COOK

THANK YOU BILLY. I WANT TO MAKE A PROMISE TO THE AUSTRALIAN PEOPLE HERE AND NOW TO BRING CHANGE TO THIS COUNTRY.

HUGHES

YES, YOU CAN BEGIN FORMING YOUR CABINET FROM YOUR SENATE MINORITY AS SOON AS POSSIBLE.

COOK

EXCUSE ME?

HUGHES

THE OFFICIAL LET US KNOW FIRST. DESPITE LOSING, LABOUR HAS
MANAGED TO RETAIN A MAJORITY OF THE SENATE, BUT I DO NOT THINK
THAT WILL MATTER. I AM SURE THEY WILL RESPECT YOU FOR THE KIND
OF MAN YOU ARE.

COOK

WHICH IS?

HUGHES

A GOOD MAN. AN HONEST MAN WHO SPEAKS HIS MIND. I AM SURE YOU
AND YOUR WIFE WILL AGREE THAT THERE HAS BEEN DECEPTION USED IN
POLITICS FOR TOO LONG.

MARY

ABSOLUTELY. IT IS TIME THE PEOPLE OF AUSTRALIA HAD A LEADER
THAT REPRESENTED HUMAN VIRTUES, SUCH AS HONESTY AND THE
WILLINGNESS TO DO THE RIGHT THING.

(EXEUNT)

ACT III

SCENE 1

(THE AUSTRALIAN PARLIAMENT. THE POLITICIANS HAVE GATHERED. FISHER AND HUGHES ARE AMONG THEM, LYNE IS ABSENT IN THIS SCENE AGAIN. ENTER COOK TOWARDS THE MIDDLE OF THE GATHERING. HE STANDS TO ADDRESS THE AWAITING CROWD.)

COOK

MEMBERS OF PARLIAMENT. I COME BEFORE YOU TODAY NOT ONLY AS YOUR PRIME MINISTER, BUT AS A VERY PROUD MAN. THE RESPONSIBILITY BESTOWED UPON ME I WILL REALISE IN GOVERNMENT AS A MOVEMENT FOR THE PEOPLE; BEGINNING BY RECOMMISSIONING THE AUSTRALIAN NAVY.

(POLITICIANS NODDING IN AGREEMENT)

HUGHES

I AGREE WITH THE PRIME MINISTER, ALTHOUGH I MUST ADVISE THAT WE CONTINUE TO BUILD UP THE FLEETS. AUSTRALIA IS A PROUD COUNTRY. IT IS OUR COUNTRY AND WE MUST PROTECT IT.

COOK

IN TIMES OF NEED, AUSTRALIA WILL REQUIRE A DEFENCE FORCE. AS MUCH AS I WISH FOR A WORLD WITHOUT VIOLENCE, BUILDING THIS NAVAL FLEET HAS LED ME TO A REALISATION. IT IS THE SMALL ACTS THAT ARE NECESSARY TO PREVENT LARGER SCALE EVENTS. WAR AND CONFLICT DEVASTATE OUR WORLD AND WE MUST NOT INVITE IT TO OUR DOORSTEP. WE MUST VOTE ON WHETHER TO EXPAND THE NAVY AS A FORCE FOR PEACE. WHO IS FOR THIS MOVEMENT?

(THERE IS AN OVERWHELMING SHOW OF HANDS)

HUGHES

THE MOTION IS OVERWHELMINGLY CARRIED IN FAVOUR PRIME MINISTER. WILL THERE BE ANYTHING ELSE BEFORE PARLIAMENT IS ADJOURNED?

COOK

YES. MY ATTORNEY GENERAL, SIR WILLIAM IRVINE GIVES HIS
APOLOGIES FOR NOT BEING HERE AND ON HIS BEHALF I WOULD LIKE TO
INTRODUCE A PROHIBITION BILL ON GOVERNMENT PREFERENTIAL
SPENDING.

FISHER

AND WHAT DOES THIS BILL ENTAIL, PRIME MINISTER?

COOK

THE BILL PROPOSES TO ABOLISH THE DIVIDE THAT HAS BEEN SET UP
FOR TOO LONG BETWEEN THE PEOPLE AND THE GOVERNMENT.

(A ROW BREAKS OUT)

FISHER

THIS IS OUTRAGEOUS!

COOK

LOOK FISHER, WE CANNOT ALLOW OURSELVES TO TAKE PREFERENTIAL
TREATMENT ABOVE THE PUBLIC. OTHERWISE HOW WILL THEY EVER BEGIN
TO RESPECT US?

HUGHES

PERHAPS BUT WE MUST BE CAREFUL. WE ARE DIFFERENT TO THE PUBLIC
AFTER ALL.

COOK

THEN LET US VOTE. WHO BELIEVES THAT THIS BILL SHOULD BE PASSED?

(VERY FEW HANDS GO UP)

AND AGAINST?

(THE REST OF THE HANDS GO UP. FISHER AND HUGHES ARE AMONG THESE HANDS.)

THE BILL IS DENIED THEN. PARLIAMENT IS ADJOURNED.

(EXIT POLITICIANS AND HUGHES)

FISHER

SUCH A PITY. IT APPEARS THE SENATE DOES NOT AGREE WITH YOUR DECISIONS. PERHAPS YOU ARE NOT AS SMART AS EVERYONE BELIEVES, COOK.

(COOK TURNS TO FISHER)

COOK

YOU KNOW AS WELL AS I DO FISHER THAT I AM JUST AS SMART AS YOU. MARY WAS RIGHT. I KNOW YOU HAVE YOUR DIRTY HAND IN ALL THIS, BUT SABOTAGE HAS NEVER BEEN YOUR FORTE.

FISHER

I ADMIT, I AM NOT ONE FOR SABOTAGING A WORTHY OPPONENT. I WOULD SOONER DEFEAT THEM IN DEBATE. BUT YOU ARE DIFFERENT JOSEPH. YOU ARE A DANGEROUS MAN WITH DANGEROUS POLICIES, SO I DID WHAT I COULD TO STOP YOU.

COOK

YOU WENT TO LYNE FOR HELP. YOU COULD NEVER HAVE ACHIEVED SOMETHING AS UNDERHANDED AS THIS BY YOURSELF.

FISHER

HE SHARED HIS HATRED OF YOU WITH ME, ALONG WITH A GREAT MANY OTHER THINGS. LYNE WANTED YOU GONE JOSEPH AND I WAS ONLY TOO HAPPY TO HELP HIM. BUT HE DOES NOT MATTER ANYMORE. I GOT WHAT I WANTED ANYWAY. I OWN THE SENATE MAJORITY, SO YOUR TITLE MEANS NOTHING. YOU ARE POWERLESS.

COOK

YOU WILL BE BROUGHT TO ACCOUNT FOR WHAT YOU HAVE DONE, YOU SNAKE.

FISHER

AT LEAST I AM DOING WHAT IS BEST FOR MY COUNTRY.

COOK

WHERE IS LYNE? I MUST SPEAK WITH HIM!

FISHER

I COULD NOT CARE LESS. HE OUTLIVED HIS USE TO ME, THEN VANISHED. IF YOU WANT TO FIND HIM YOU WILL HAVE TO LOOK YOURSELF.

COOK

THERE IS ONLY ONE PLACE HE COULD BE. I KNOW WHERE HE IS.

(EXEUNT)

ACT III

SCENE 2

(LYNE'S HOUSE IN DOUBLE BAY. HE IS BEDRIDDEN AND COUGHING. HE IS IN SERIOUS PAIN. THERE IS A KNOCK AT THE DOOR. ENTER COOK.)

LYNE

COOK. IS THAT YOU? IN MY WEAKENED STATE I CANNOT TELL FOR SURE.

COOK

YES WILLIAM. I AM HERE. I CAME TO SEE YOU.

LYNE

DID YOU KNOW OF MY ILLNESS?

COOK

I SUSPECTED AS MUCH. YOUR ABSENCE IN PARLIAMENT HAS CERTAINLY BEEN NOTICED.

LYNE

WHY WOULD THE PRIME MINISTER WANT TO LISTEN TO ME? I AM THE LAST OF THE PROTECTIONISTS, AND YET YOU HAVE STILL COME.

COOK

I SEE YOU ARE STILL AS STUBBORN AS EVER WILLIAM. ILLNESS NEVER DID HAVE AN EFFECT ON YOUR PERSONALITY.

(LYNE COUGHS)

LYNE

NO. IT NEVER DID. BUT MY AGE, IT SEEMS, HAS CAUGHT UP WITH ME.

COOK

YOU LOOK ILL, BUT YOU DO NOT LOOK OLD. I WOULD NOT BE SO HARD ON YOURSELF. I CAME TO WISH YOU A SWIFT RECOVERY OLD FRIEND, AND LOOK FORWARD TO SEEING YOU BACK IN PARLIAMENT.

LYNE

I ADMIRE YOUR THINKING, BUT I AM AFRAID THIS MAY BE MY FINAL HOUR.

COOK

WHAT?

LYNE

MY GOUT HAS CAUGHT UP WITH ME. I AM WEAKENED BY INFECTION AND THE DOCTOR SAYS I DO NOT HAVE LONG TO LIVE.

COOK

I AM SORRY WILLIAM. I DO NOT KNOW WHAT TO SAY. TRUTHFULLY I HAVE NEVER BEEN GOOD IN THESE SITUATIONS. MY FATHER DIED WHEN I WAS VERY YOUNG. ALL I COULD DO WAS BURY MY SADNESS, AND I FOUND SOLACE IN RELIGION AND KNOWLEDGE. I SUPPOSE I NEVER REALLY GOT OVER HIS DEATH. I STILL THINK ABOUT HIM EVERY DAY.

LYNE

YOU HAVE NEVER APPEARED AS A WEAK MAN TO ME JOSEPH. THAT IS WHY IT WAS SO DIFFICULT TO DECEIVE YOU.

COOK

YOU HAVE COST ME A LOT AS PRIME MINISTER LYNE. YOU DECEIVE ME ON A REGULAR BASIS. BUT I SUPPOSE THAT HAS BECOME THE NATURE OF OUR FRIENDSHIP.

LYNE

YES, BUT THIS TIME I SHALL HAVE THE LAST LAUGH. FISHER WAS
JUST A PAWN IN MY GRAND SCHEME. I NEEDED SOMEONE TO TAKE THE
FALL ONCE YOU BECAME PRIME MINISTER. HE NEVER REALLY MATTERED.
IT WAS ABOUT THE ELECTION YOU SEE. I COULD NOT STAND TO SEE
YOUR IDIOTIC PHILOSOPHIES INFECT MY BEAUTIFUL COUNTRY. SO I
TOLD FISHER TO STAND AGAINST YOU KNOWING HE WOULD LOSE.

COOK

I KNOW YOU WILLIAM. YOU ALWAYS THINK THREE MOVES AHEAD AND
THERE IS ALWAYS A CATCH.

LYNE

OH THERE IS. AND WHAT A CATCH IT WAS. I BRIBED THEM JOSEPH. I
BRIBED THEM ALL. SOME OF THE SENATE MEMBERS DID NOT TAKE WHAT
I GAVE THEM, BUT I GAINED INFLUENCE OVER ENOUGH OF THEM TO
ESTABLISH A MAJORITY IN THE SENATE FOR LABOUR.

COOK

BUT YOU ARE A PROTECTIONIST WILLIAM. I UNDERSTAND WHY YOU
INITIALLY SIDED WITH FISHER, BUT THIS IS NOT YOUR STYLE. YOU
NEVER TAKE ANY CHANCES UNLESS YOU CAN PERSONALLY GAIN FROM IT.

LYNE

IT IS TRUE THAT I HAD NOTHING TO GAIN. BUT I WOULD RATHER SEE
YOUR LITTLE FREE TRADE UTOPIA FALL INTO RUIN THAN PROFIT AT
ALL FROM THIS ENDEAVOUR.

COOK

YOU SACRIFICED YOUR ENTIRE IDEOLOGY TO DESTROY MY DREAM!

LYNE

AND IT WAS WORTH IT JOSEPH. IT WAS WORTH IT IN EVERY WAY. FOR A DYING MAN, IT IS A DREAM COME TRUE. I WOULD RATHER DIE, KNOWING I HAVE TAKEN YOU DOWN WITH ME THAN SEE YOU SUCCEED AND LIVE.

(LYNE SMILES GLEEFULLY)

COOK

IT IS DONE. ALTHOUGH I CAN NEVER FORGIVE YOU FOR WHAT YOU DID, THERE IS SOMEONE WHO WILL. I AM SURE THE LORD WILL FORGIVE YOUR SINS, THOUGH IT MAY TAKE HIM A WHILE.

LYNE

(LAUGHS)

PERHAPS HE WILL. PERHAPS HE WILL.

(LYNE DRIFTS OFF INTO DEATH. COOK KNEELS BESIDE THE BED.)

COOK

YOU WERE TRULY A FALLEN ANGEL WILLIAM. I WILL CHOOSE TO REMEMBER YOU AS YOU ONCE WERE, NOT THE MAN YOU BECAME.

(COOK STANDS. HE TURNS TO GO.)

MAY THE BLESSING OF THE LORD BE UPON YOU FOREVER WILLIAM. AMEN.

(EXEUNT)

ACT III

SCENE 3

(THE COOK HOUSEHOLD. THE CHILDREN ARE PLAYING GAMES AND JOSEPH IS IN HIS STUDY. ENTER MARY.)

MARY

HELLO EVERYBODY, I AM HOME!

CHILD 2

MOTHER!

MARY

HELLO SWEETHEART. HOW ARE YOU?

CHILD 2

I HAVE BEEN HAVING THE MOST WONDERFUL DAY. FATHER PLAYED A GAME WITH US WHILE YOU WERE OUT. HOW IS UNCLE WILLIAM?

MARY

MY BROTHER IS VERY WELL. HOW IS YOUR FATHER? IS HE FARING ANY BETTER THAN THIS MORNING?

CHILD 2

HE APPEARS TO BE VERY GLUM BUT I DO NOT KNOW WHY. HE HAS BEEN PLAYING WITH US ALL DAY.

MARY

BEING THE PRIME MINISTER OF A COUNTRY HAS CERTAIN RESPONSIBILITIES. JUST BE GLAD THAT HE IS ABLE TO SPEND ANY TIME WITH YOU AT ALL.

CHILD 2

BUT WHY IS HE SAD?

MARY

YOUR FATHER HAS A LOT ON HIS MIND AT THE MOMENT. I NEED TO
TALK TO HIM, WHERE IS HE?

CHILD 2

IN HIS STUDY.

(MARY WALKS OVER TOWARDS COOK. THE CHILDREN RESUME PLAYING.)

MARY

HELLO JOSEPH, HOW ARE YOU FEELING?

COOK

I THOUGHT A DAY AT HOME WITH THE CHILDREN WOULD CHEER ME UP
AFTER EVERYTHING THAT HAS HAPPENED.

MARY

IT IS NATURAL TO FEEL THIS WAY AFTER SUCH A LOSS.

COOK

PERHAPS, BUT LYNE STILL PLAYED ME FOR A FOOL AND I WAS NAÏVE
ENOUGH TO BELIEVE THAT HE WOULD STAY OUT OF MY AFFAIRS.

MARY

HE WAS A POLITICIAN JOSEPH, AND A SHIFTY ONE AT THAT.

COOK

YOU DID NOT HEAR WHAT HE SAID TO ME MARY. HE TOLD ME HE WOULD RATHER DIE THAN SEE ME SUCCEED. HE BECAME SO OBSESSED WITH STOPPING ME THAT HE WAS IGNORING HIS HEALTH. AND NOW I FEEL NOTHING BUT GUILT.

MARY

I SEE NO REASON WHY YOU SHOULD FEEL GUILTY JOSEPH. WE ARE FREE TO LIVE OUR LIVES HOWEVER WE CHOOSE, AND LYNE CHOSE TO OBSESS OVER PROBLEMS THAT HE CREATED IN HIS OWN HEAD.

COOK

TO SEE MY FRIEND LIVE AND DIE IN SUCH AN AGONISING WAY THOUGH. THE STRESS OF THIS JOB IS BEGINNING TO TAKE ITS TOLL. LYNE AND FISHER HAVE PUT ME IN A POSITION WHERE I CANNOT EFFECTIVELY MAKE DECISIONS IN PARLIAMENT.

MARY

WHY IS THAT?

COOK

LABOUR HAS A MAJORITY IN THE SENATE. I CANNOT PASS ANY LAWS WITHOUT THEIR AUTHORITY.

(MARY LOOKS SHOCKED)

THIS IS WHY I HAVE NOT BEEN ABLE TO LIVE UP TO MANY OF MY PROMISES. BECAUSE AS A DEMOCRATIC SOCIETY, WE VOTED NOT TO PROGRESS OURSELVES. I ONLY WISH THE OTHER MEMBERS OF THE SENATE ARE ABLE TO SEE THIS.

MARY

I NEVER REALISED YOU HAD SUCH A TOUGH JOB JOSEPH. I THOUGHT YOUR FIGHT AGAINST THE ODDS ENDED WHEN YOU BECAME PRIME MINISTER.

COOK

THERE IS NOTHING I CAN DO. LYNE WAS A VERY SMART MAN AND HE USED THE SYSTEM AGAINST ME. NEVERTHELESS, I HAVE A COUNTRY TO GOVERN AND I MUST DO SO TO THE BEST OF MY ABILITY. AUSTRALIA MUST HAVE A STRONG GOVERNMENT AND IT IS MY RESPONSIBILITY TO MAKE THAT HAPPEN.

MARY

THIS COUNTRY NEEDS A GOOD MAN, A GOOD LEADER, AND THAT IS EXACTLY WHAT YOU ARE JOSEPH. YOU JUST NEED TO BE CONFIDENT IN YOURSELF.

COOK

SOMETHING NEEDS TO CHANGE, OTHERWISE I BELIEVE IT WILL TEAR PARLIAMENT APART FROM THE INSIDE. BUT I BELIEVE IN THE SYSTEM, AND IN GOVERNMENT. AND IN THE PEOPLE OF AUSTRALIA.

MARY

WE HAVE BOTH HAD A LONG DAY. YOU CONTEMPLATING YOUR DUTIES AND I AT THE RED CROSS. HOPEFULLY THINGS WILL WORK OUT FOR THE BEST JOSEPH. I BELIEVE IN YOU.

(THEY KISS. EXEUNT)

ACT III

SCENE 4

(1914. THE AUSTRALIAN PARLIAMENT IS ONSTAGE. HUGHES AND FISHER HAVE GATHERED WITH THEM.)

FISHER

WHY HAS COOK CALLED THIS EMERGENCY MEETING OF PARLIAMENT?

HUGHES

I DO NOT KNOW FISHER. WHEN I LAST HEARD FROM JOSEPH HE SOUNDED TRULY AFRAID. I HOPE HE IS ALRIGHT.

FISHER

BE WARY OF COOK BILLY. HE IS LIKE FIRE. IF YOU GET TOO CLOSE TO HIM YOU WILL GO UP IN FLAMES.

HUGHES

HE IS A GOOD MAN FISHER AND I WISH YOU COULD RESPECT HIM FOR THAT AS I DO. BUT JUST BECAUSE I RESPECT HIM DOES NOT MEAN I BELIEVE IN HIS IDEALS.

FISHER

HE IS BAD NEWS BILLY. REMEMBER THAT AND HE WILL NOT CORRUPT YOU.

(ENTER COOK)

HUGHES

CORRUPT?

COOK

MEMBERS OF PARLIAMENT. I AM SORRY FOR ARRIVING SO LATE, BUT I HAVE ONLY JUST RETURNED FROM VICTORIA.

126

HUGHES

PRIME MINISTER, WHY HAVE YOU CALLED THIS EMERGENCY MEETING OF PARLIAMENT? WE ALL HAVE JOBS TO DO AND WOULD LIKE TO KNOW WHY YOU HAVE SUMMONED US.

(COOK SIGHS AND LOWERS HIS HEAD)

COOK

I HAVE CALLED YOU ALL HERE TODAY BECAUSE… BECAUSE I HAVE RECEIVED A DISPATCH FROM THE IMPERIAL GOVERNMENT BACK IN ENGLAND. IT IS WITH A HEAVY HEART THAT I MUST ANNOUNCE TO YOU ALL; WAR HAS BROKEN OUT IN EUROPE.

(SOME OF THE POLITICIANS ARE SHOCKED, OTHERS NOT SO MUCH.)

HUGHES

WAR? I AM NOT SURPRISED, THE TENSION HAS BEEN MOUNTING BETWEEN THE POWERS IN EUROPE FOR MANY YEARS NOW. I FEARED THAT SOMETHING LIKE THIS WOULD HAPPEN.

COOK

THIS IS UNLIKE ANYTHING I HAVE EVER WITNESSED BEFORE. THE TENSION BETWEEN THE POWERS HAS CAUSED THE SURROUNDING NATIONS TO BE PULLED INTO THE CONFLICT.

HUGHES

BUT DOES THAT MEAN WE SHOULD GO TO WAR AS WELL?

COOK

AS MUCH AS I WOULD LIKE TO AVOID THIS CATASTROPHE HUGHES, I FEAR THIS WILL BE IMPOSSIBLE. THE IMPERIAL GOVERNMENT HAS SENT THIS MESSAGE OUT TO ALL OF THE COLONIES.

127

FISHER

IF THAT IS THE CASE THEN WE MUST ANSWER THE CALL. HOW MANY OF US HAVE EMIGRATED FROM BRITAIN? I WOULD WAGER THAT MOST OF THIS PARLIAMENT WAS BORN BACK HOME AMONG THE HILLS AND IN THE CITIES OF ENGLAND.

COOK

FISHER IS RIGHT! WE MAY NOT LIVE IN ENGLAND ANY LONGER, BUT IN OUR HEARTS IT IS STILL OUR HOME.

FISHER

WE HAVE AN OBLIGATION TO STAND BESIDE OUR BROTHERS IN BATTLE.

COOK

AUSTRALIA WILL JOIN THE WAR EFFORT TO HELP DEFEND OUR MOTHER NATION FROM THE ONCOMING GERMAN THREAT. WE SHARE A BROTHERHOOD WITH THE REST OF THE BRITISH EMPIRE. FISHER SAYS WE HAVE AN OBLIGATION TO HELP OUR BROTHERS, I BELIEVE IT RUNS DEEPER THAN THAT. I BELIEVE WE HAVE A DUTY TO DEFEND OUR BROTHERS, AND HONOUR THEM LIKE WE WOULD WITH GOD. I HAVE COME TO REALISE OVER THE PAST FEW DAYS THAT AUSTRALIA WILL INEVITABLY BE DRAGGED INTO THE CONFLICT. SO WE MUST GO FORTH AND JOIN OF OUR OWN VOLITION.

(PARLIAMENT ERUPTS IN APPLAUSE. EXIT COOK AND POLITICIANS.)

FISHER

COOK IS BECOMING OVERWHELMED. I CAN SEE IT. EVERY DAY HE HAS MORE WORK TO DO. BILLY, WE CAN USE HIS WEAKNESS TO REGAIN POWER.

HUGHES

FISHER, WAR HAS COME TO EUROPE. I THINK WE HAVE BIGGER PRIORITIES THAN WORRYING ABOUT THE POLICIES OF THE PRIME MINISTER.

(EXIT HUGHES)

128

FISHER

COWARD! YOU ARE JUST AS WEAK!

(EXEUNT)

ACT III

SCENE 5

(THE COOK HOUSEHOLD. COOK IS AT HIS DESK SWAMPED WITH PAPERS. HE IS EXHAUSTED BUT STILL WORKING.)

COOK

I CANNOT KEEP WORKING LIKE THIS. WHEN I TAKE ONE STEP TOWARDS MY GOALS I AM PUSHED TWO STEPS BACK BY PARLIAMENT.

(COOK COLLAPSES ONTO THE DESK WITH EXHAUSTION. ENTER MARY.)

MARY

(SIGHS)

JOSEPH. MUST YOU CARE SO MUCH ABOUT OUR COUNTRY?

(SHE STROKES THE TOP OF HIS HEAD. COOK BEGINS TO WAKE UP.)

COOK

MARY? IS THAT YOU?

MARY

YOU FELL ASLEEP JOSEPH. IT HAS BEEN THE THIRD TIME THIS WEEK.

COOK

I HAVE A LOT OF WORK TO DO MARY. I AM THE PRIME MINISTER OF AUSTRALIA.

MARY

EVEN PRIME MINISTERS NEED TO REST EVERY ONCE IN A WHILE JOSEPH. YOU ARE HARDLY EATING, YOU ARE BARELY SLEEPING AND IT WORRIES ME.

COOK

YOU MUST UNDERSTAND MARY. I MUST KEEP WORKING. THE WAR HAS BEEN VERY TAXING ON AUSTRALIA, AND THE SENATE STILL REFUSES TO BACK MY PRINCIPLES OF FREE TRADE. I MUST BRING CHANGE TO THIS COUNTRY, BUT I HAVE VERY LITTLE DEMOCRATIC AUTHORITY TO DO SO.

MARY

IF YOU DO NOT STOP JOSEPH YOU WILL WORK YOURSELF TO DEATH.

COOK

RUBBISH! THIS IS VERY IMPORTANT WORK THAT NEEDS TO BE DONE AND IF IT IS TO BE DONE, I MUST WORK HARDER.

MARY

THERE IS A DIFFERENCE BETWEEN WORKING HARD AND WORKING YOURSELF INTO THE GROUND. COME ON JOSEPH, I WILL HELP YOU TO BED. YOUR HEAD WILL BE CLEARER IN THE MORNING.

(COOK IS HELPED TO HIS FEET BY MARY. HE STRETCHES AND YAWNS.)

COOK

I DO NOT NEED TO REST MARY. I AM PERFECTLY FINE.

MARY

NO JOSEPH. YOU NEED SLEEP. YOU CANNOT KEEP WORKING AND WORKING UNTIL YOU DROP. IT WILL NOT HELP YOU AND I WILL NOT ALLOW YOU TO DO SO.

COOK

WHAT ABOUT OUR SON MARY? DO YOU THINK GEORGE IS RESTING? NO, HE IS WORKING AND FIGHTING TO SECURE WORLDWIDE PEACE.

MARY

GEORGE MAY BE FIGHTING FOR OUR FREEDOM, BUT I AM SURE THAT HE NEVER FORGETS TO EAT AND TO SLEEP EVERY ONCE IN A WHILE. NOW COME ON JOSEPH, THIS IS GETTING RIDICULOUS.

COOK

ALRIGHT MARY. I WILL GET SOME REST. I WANT YOU TO KNOW THAT I AM ONLY THINKING ABOUT THE FUTURE OF OUR COUNTRY. AND YOU.

(MARY SMILES SWEETLY)

MARY

TOMORROW IS ANOTHER DAY, AND WHEN THAT DAY COMES YOU WILL KNOW WHAT TO DO. YOU ALWAYS DO.

(EXEUNT)

ACT III

SCENE 6

(THE AUSTRALIAN PARLIAMENT. COOK IS ONSTAGE. ENTER POLITICIANS, HUGHES AND FISHER.)

COOK

THANK YOU ALL FOR COMING TODAY. CONTRARY TO OUR PREVIOUS MEETING WE SHALL NOT BE DISCUSSING MATTERS OF THE WAR EFFORT TODAY. THERE ARE MUCH BIGGER ISSUES WHICH I MUST ADDRESS FIRST.

HUGHES

BUT WE MUST CONTINUE TO DEBATE THE POSSIBILITIES OF CONSCRIPTION PRIME MINISTER. EVERY DAY MORE AND MORE TROOPS ARE KILLED ON ALL FRONTS. WE CANNOT TAKE A BACKSEAT TO ADDRESS OTHER ISSUES AT SUCH A CRITICAL TIME.

COOK

SETTLE DOWN HUGHES. WE MUST DO SO. I HAVE TRIED TO GOVERN THIS COUNTRY IN PERHAPS ITS DARKEST HOUR, BUT I CANNOT DO THIS TO THE BEST OF MY ABILITY. EVERY DECISION I TRY TO MAKE IS SHOT DOWN.

FISHER

THE SENATE HAVE THEIR OWN REASONS NOT TO PURSUE YOUR PHILOSOPHIES COOK. PERHAPS THEY SEE THEM AS FANTASIES.

COOK

PERHAPS. PERHAPS NOT. NEVERTHELESS, I PROMISED CHANGE AND CALLED FOR PROGRESSION. THAT IS WHY TODAY, I AM CALLING FOR A DISSOLUTION OF PARLIAMENT. EFFECTIVE IMMEDIATELY I AM NO LONGER YOUR PRIME MINISTER.

(GASPS AND WHISPERS COME FROM THE POLITICIANS)

133

HUGHES

WHO WILL LEAD OUR COUNTRY? WE ARE IN AN HOUR OF NEED JOSEPH!
YOU CANNOT AFFORD TO RESIGN.

COOK

IF WE WISH TO PROGRESS AS A COUNTRY, THEN I CAN NO LONGER BE
PRIME MINISTER.

FISHER

I ALWAYS KNEW YOU WERE A WEAK LEADER COOK. IT IS SO GOOD OF
YOU TO PROVE ME RIGHT.

COOK

I DO NOT RESPECT YOU FISHER. ESPECIALLY AFTER EVERYTHING YOU
AND LYNE HAVE DONE TO ME. BUT FOR THIS COUNTRY TO MOVE FORWARD
IT NEEDS A STRONG LEADER. WE MUST MAKE WAR ON GERMANY AND NOT
OURSELVES. WHICH IS WHY I AM CONCEDING THE POSITION OF PRIME
MINISTER TO YOU.

FISHER

I WOULD ACCEPT THIS GRACIOUS HONOUR WITH OPEN ARMS, BUT I
CANNOT. I HAVE BEEN OFFERED THE POSITION OF HIGH COMMISSIONER
IN LONDON. YET I CANNOT ALLOW THE LABOUR PARTY TO CONCEDE
POWER TO THE COMMONWEALTH LIBERALS, SO I GRANT THE POSITION OF
PRIME MINISTER TO MY EVER FAITHFUL RIGHT HAND MAN WILLIAM
HUGHES.

(HUGHES STANDS UP)

HUGHES

I ACCEPT THIS POSITION WITH PRIDE. UNLIKE YOU, I AM NO COWARD, FISHER.

(FISHER LOOKS SHOCKED)

AS MY FIRST ACT AS PRIME MINISTER, I MOVE THAT FORMER PRIME MINISTER JOSEPH COOK BE ALLOWED TO FINISH WHAT HE STARTED WITH THE AUSTRALIAN NAVY.

FISHER

YOU TURNCOAT! I AM NO COWARD HUGHES! WHEN I RETURN TO LONDON I WILL SEE THAT YOUR CAREER IS RUINED!

HUGHES

YOU WOULD HAVE TO GO THROUGH HIS MAJESTY TO DO SO FISHER. I AM CERTAIN HE WOULD BACK ME, AS I AM NOW IN CHARGE OF THE AUSTRALIAN WAR EFFORT. MEMBERS OF PARLIAMENT, HEAR ME NOW. JOSEPH COOK IS THE BEST MAN FOR THE JOB AND I HAVE COMPLETE FAITH IN HIS ABILITY TO HELP OUR WAR EFFORT IN EVERY WAY HE CAN. WHAT SAY YOU?

(THE MEMBERS OF PARLIAMENT RAISE THEIR HANDS EXCEPT FISHER)

FISHER

NO! THIS CANNOT BE HAPPENING!

HUGHES

YOU HAVE NO JURISDICTION HERE FISHER. NOW LEAVE, YOU HAVE IMPORTANT WORK TO DO IN ENGLAND. AS FOR THE REST OF THE COUNTRY, I EXPECT EVERY MAN AND WOMAN FROM THIS DAY FORTH TO DO THEIR DUTY, WHETHER IT BE HELPING THE SICK AND WOUNDED OR FIGHTING ABROAD IN EUROPE. THAT IS WHY I AM INTRODUCING CONSCRIPTION FOR EVERY MAN AT THE AGE OF EIGHTEEN AND ABOVE. WE MUST REPEL THE GERMAN MENACE WITH THE UTMOST INTENT!

(FISHER LEAVES, FUMING. POLITICIANS CHEER. EXIT POLITICIANS.)

COOK

BILLY. WHY DID YOU STAND UP FOR ME?

HUGHES

I THOUGHT IT WAS ABOUT TIME SOMEONE STOOD UP TO FISHER. HE REALLY CAN BE A BULLY WHEN HE WANTS TO BE.

COOK

THAT IS THE NATURE OF POLITICS I SUPPOSE. AS IN CHESS, ONE MOMENT YOU ARE AN ALL POWERFUL QUEEN, THE NEXT YOU ARE NOTHING MORE THAN A LOWLY PAWN.

HUGHES

IT IS A TOUGH WORLD, BUT WE CAN FIX IT. WE MUST AID OUR ALLIES, STARTING WITH CONSCRIPTION AND BY STRENGTHENING THE NAVY. THE NAVY IS YOUR PROJECT JOSEPH. I HAVE THE UTMOST FAITH THAT YOU WILL DELIVER A POWERFUL NAVY FOR US TO HELP THE ALLIES IN BATTLE.

COOK

THANK YOU BILLY. I WILL NOT LET YOU DOWN.

HUGHES

FINISH WHAT YOU STARTED MY FRIEND. GOOD LUCK.

(EXEUNT)

ACT III

SCENE 7

(A FEW EXTRAS ARE ONSTAGE. ENTER COOK.)

COOK

MEN, YOU ARE THE NEW RECRUITS FOR THE AUSTRALIAN NAVY. MAKE NO MISTAKE, THIS IS NOT AN EASY JOB. WHILE THE MILITARY CONTINUES TO FIGHT OVERSEAS, OUR JOB IS TO MAKE SURE THEY GET TO ALL WAR FRONTS AS WELL AS PROTECTING OUR OWN. ANY QUESTIONS?

RECRUIT 1

ARE THE RUMOURS TRUE MINISTER?

COOK

DESPITE WHAT YOU MAY HAVE HEARD IN THE PAST, THE AUSTRALIAN NAVY WAS FOUNDED BY ME, JOSEPH COOK. EVERY MAN WHO STEPS FORWARD I AM HONOURED TO ENLIST BECAUSE UNLIKE THE MILITARY WE ARE THE TRUE HEART AND SOUL OF THE AUSTRALIAN PEACEKEEPING FORCE.

RECRUIT 2

WHEN WILL WE RECEIVE OUR TRAINING?

COOK

YOU CERTAINLY ARE EAGER TO SERVE YOUR COUNTRY. I SHALL NOT DISAPPOINT YOU. ONCE YOU ARE ALL FULLY TRAINED AND READY TO ENTER COMBAT, YOUR FIRST MISSION WILL BE TO TRAVEL TO GERMAN NEW GUINEA. THERE IS A WIRELESS COMMUNICATIONS CENTRE WHICH THE GERMANS ARE USING TO CUT OFF OUR TRANSMISSIONS TO ENGLAND. YOU WILL BE JOINED BY OTHER RECRUITS ON YOUR MISSION TO DESTROY THIS FACILITY FOR THE BENEFIT OF THE BRITISH EMPIRE. AFTER YOU HAVE COMPLETED YOUR MISSION, WAIT FOR FURTHER ORDERS FROM THE BRITISH NAVAL COMMAND. THEY WILL SEND YOU EVERYTHING YOU NEED TO KNOW. IS EVERYBODY READY TO BEGIN THEIR TRAINING?

RECRUITS
(*TOGETHER*)

YES MINISTER!

(*EXEUNT*)

ACT III

SCENE 8

(THE AUSTRALIAN RED CROSS, 1915. MARY IS HELPING THE SICK AND WOUNDED.)

MARY

(TO WOUNDED SOLDIER)

I WOULD NOT WORRY TOO MUCH. WITH SOME GOOD LUCK YOU WILL BE BACK ON YOUR FEET IN NO TIME. YOU JUST NEED TO REST THE WOUND FOR NOW.

(ENTER COOK)

COOK

MARY I MUST SPEAK WITH YOU.

MARY

I CANNOT TALK NOW JOSEPH. I HAVE LOTS OF PATIENTS TO TAKE CARE OF.

COOK

I AM PLEASED THAT YOU WANT TO HELP, BUT YOU ARE NOT A DOCTOR MARY.

MARY

PERHAPS NOT, BUT A WILLING PAIR OF HANDS NEVER DID ANY HARM. BESIDES, I HAVE BEEN LEARNING FROM THE FEW PROFESSIONALS THAT ARE WORKING HERE.

COOK

YES I CAN SEE. BUT WE NEED TO TALK.

MARY

WHAT ABOUT? I AM ALREADY DOING AS MUCH WORK AS I CAN TO HELP.

COOK

YES. YOU ARE A VITAL ASSET IN THESE TROUBLED TIMES, BUT MARY COOK CANNOT TAKE ON GERMANY ALL BY HERSELF.

MARY

I WOULD NOT DREAM OF IT, THOUGH I FEEL I COULD DO SO.

COOK

WE NEED TO SEND MORE TROOPS TO HELP OUR ALLIES IN BATTLE. MORE AND MORE ARE DYING EVERY DAY.

MARY

I KNOW. I WORRY FOR OUR SON EVERY DAY CONSTANTLY IN FEAR THAT HIS LATEST LETTER FROM GALLIPOLI WILL BE HIS LAST.

COOK

THIS IS HARD TO SAY BUT, WE HAVE BEEN SUCCESSFUL IN OUR ENDEAVOUR TO INTRODUCE CONSCRIPTION LAWS.

MARY

WHAT!? HOW COULD YOU LET THIS HAPPEN? I DO NOT WANT MY CHILDREN BEING FORCED INTO COMBAT!

COOK

I AM SORRY MARY, BUT THIS DECISION WAS INEVITABLE. I DO NOT LIKE IT ANY MORE THAN YOU DO. THE REALITY IS THAT WE ARE STRUGGLING IN THIS WAR AND EVERYONE NEEDS TO DO THEIR DUTY. WE ARE ONLY MAKING THIS OFFICIAL.

MARY

BUT OUR SONS JOSEPH. THEY ARE STILL ONLY BOYS, BARELY MEN AT ALL. AND NOW YOU EXPECT THEM TO GO TO WAR AND DIE FOR THEIR COUNTRY? NO! I REFUSE TO LET THIS HAPPEN!

COOK

NOW YOU LISTEN TO ME MARY TURNER. I KNOW THINGS ARE HARD RIGHT NOW. YOU HAVE ALWAYS WANTED WHAT IS BEST FOR OUR CHILDREN, BUT OUR CHILDREN HAVE GROWN UP NOW AND YOU NEED TO REALISE THIS.

(MARY LOWERS HER HEAD)

LOOK AT ME. GEORGE IS STILL ALIVE. HOLD ONTO THAT AND TRUST THAT EVERYTHING OUR GOVERNMENT DOES IS FOR THE GREATER GOOD OF THE ALLIES. TRUST ME, CONSCRIPTION WILL END THIS WAR MORE QUICKLY.

MARY

IF THEY GO, WILL YOU PRAY FOR THEIR SAFETY?

COOK

I PRAY FOR OUR CHILDREN TO BE SAFE EVERY NIGHT MARY. BUT WHAT KEEPS ME CALM IS THAT I KNOW THEY ARE CAPABLE ENOUGH TO MAKE THEIR OWN WAYS.

(EXEUNT)

ACT III

SCENE 9

(ENGLAND, 1918. COOK AND MARY ARE TALKING AMONGST THEMSELVES.)

MARY

THIS WAR HAS GONE ON FOR SO LONG. IT FEELS AS IF IT HAS BROKEN OUR FAMILY, JOSEPH. WE ARE ALL SO FAR APART, US HERE IN ENGLAND, OUR FRIENDS BACK IN AUSTRALIA AND OUR CHILDREN SCATTERED ACROSS EUROPE.

COOK

WE ARE ALL DOING WHAT WE CAN TO TRY AND BRING PEACE. I AM PROUD TO REPRESENT AUSTRALIA AT THE IMPERIAL WAR CONFERENCE AND I COULD NOT HAVE DONE THIS WITHOUT YOUR SUPPORT.

MARY

I JUST WANT MY CHILDREN TO BE SAFE.

COOK

I KNOW. I KNOW HOW HARD IT IS NOT KNOWING WHERE THEY ARE OR WHAT IS HAPPENING TO THEM.

(ENTER HUGHES)

WHAT IS THE LATEST WORD BILLY?

HUGHES

WE DID IT JOSEPH. THE WAR IS OVER AND THE ALLIES ARE VICTORIOUS.

COOK

I NEVER THOUGHT I WOULD SEE THIS DAY.

HUGHES

ARE YOU ALRIGHT JOSEPH? YOU LOOK A LITTLE CONCERNED.

MARY

OUR SONS WENT OFF TO FIGHT IN THE WAR. WE HAVE NOT HEARD FROM
ANY OF THEM FOR SEVERAL MONTHS NOW.

COOK

YOU BOTH HAVE NOTHING TO WORRY ABOUT, I AM FINE. I JUST CANNOT
BELIEVE THE WAR IS OVER. FINALLY OUR CHILDREN CAN COME HOME,
AND AS HEROES.

HUGHES

THINGS HAVE BEEN HARD FOR MANY COUNTRIES ACROSS THE WORLD OVER
THE PAST YEARS. BUT WE NOW HAVE A CHANCE TO PUT RIGHT THE
WRONGS THAT HAVE BEEN DONE.

MARY

HOW? HOW CAN YOU PUT RIGHT THE DEATHS OF MILLIONS OF PEOPLE?

HUGHES

WE CANNOT. BUT WE CAN DO THE NEXT BEST THING. REPRESENTATIVES
FROM ALL THE ALLIED NATIONS NEED TO MEET WITH THOSE OF US WHO
HAVE BEEN WORKING TO PUT AN END TO THE GERMAN STRANGLEHOLD OF
TYRANNY IN EUROPE. ALTHOUGH WE CANNOT BRING THE DEAD BACK TO
LIFE, WE CAN ACHIEVE RETRIBUTION FOR OUR BROTHERS.

COOK

I DO NOT WISH TO FIND RETRIBUTION. I ONLY WANT THE CONFLICT TO
END.

HUGHES

DO YOU NOT FEEL THAT THEY DESERVE IT THOUGH? ON BEHALF OF ALL THE FAMILIES OF AUSTRALIA, GERMANY MUST ANSWER FOR THEIR CRIMES.

COOK

I AGREE THAT THERE MUST BE CONSEQUENCES, BUT WE MUST FIND A WAY TO REASON WITH THEM. THE GERMANS ARE STILL MEN AFTER ALL. MY FATHER WAS A VERY HARD WORKER. HE ALWAYS KEPT HIS PROMISES AND THE PEOPLE ADMIRED HIM FOR IT. IF I HAVE LEARNED ANYTHING FROM THIS, IT IS THAT BY WORKING WITH PEOPLE WE CAN EARN THAT WHICH CANNOT BE BOUGHT.

HUGHES

BUT WHAT COULD WE HOPE TO EARN FROM THE GERMANS?

COOK

PERHAPS THEIR RESPECT FOR STARTERS. THEN MAYBE WE CAN ACHIEVE A LASTING PEACE. I HAVE ALWAYS BELIEVED THAT IF I FOLLOWED THE EXAMPLE MY FATHER SET I COULD ACHIEVE GREAT THINGS.

HUGHES

YOU ARE RIGHT JOSEPH. THIS IS OUR CHANCE TO MAKE HISTORY AND RIGHT THE WRONGS OF THE PAST THROUGH NEGOTIATING A PEACEFUL SOLUTION.

COOK

IF WE ARE TRULY GOING TO WIN THIS WAR, WE MUST SHOW THE GERMANS THAT TOGETHER, WE CAN REBUILD THIS WORLD BETTER THAN BEFORE. IF WE DO NOTHING BUT DESTROY, THEN WE WILL BE LEFT WITH NOTHING BUT RUBBLE. THAT IS WHY WE MUST CREATE A LASTING PEACE WITH THE GERMANS, MY FRIEND.

HUGHES

TO THE GOODNESS OF PEOPLE AND THE ALLIED CAUSE.

(EXIT HUGHES)

COOK

CHECKMATE KAISER. CHECKMATE.

(EXEUNT)

ACT III

SCENE 10

(COOK HAS RETURNED TO ENGLAND WITH HUGHES. THEY HAVE FINISHED THE CONFERENCE AND ARE JUST COMING OUT OF THE BUILDING, WHICH IS TO ONE SIDE OF THE STAGE.)

HUGHES

I MUST SAY, THE CONFERENCE WENT A LOT BETTER THAN PLANNED.

COOK

INDEED. THE PRESIDENT WAS VERY ADAMANT ABOUT WHAT HE WANTED FROM THE GERMANS…

(SIGHS)

I HAVE MISSED THESE SHORES AND I AM DELIGHTED TO SEE THEM AGAIN.

(ENTER ARTHUR)

ARTHUR

I DOUBT THESE SHORES ARE THE ONLY THING YOU HAVE MISSED.

COOK

ARTHUR!

ARTHUR

HELLO JOSEPH, GOOD TO SEE YOU.

COOK

I SEE YOU GOT MY LETTER MY FRIEND. HOW GOES THE PROGRESS IN THE MINING INDUSTRY?

ARTHUR

VERY WELL JOSEPH, VERY WELL INDEED. BUT I DID NOT COME TO TALK ABOUT MYSELF. AS MUCH AS I WOULD LIKE TO REMINISCE ABOUT THE GOOD OLD DAYS I BRING NEWS FROM THE KING HIMSELF.

HUGHES

FROM KING GEORGE?

ARTHUR

THE VERY SAME. I DO NOT BELIEVE WE HAVE BEEN INTRODUCED. ARTHUR HASSAM, MINING ENGINEER AND CONSULTANT.

HUGHES

BILLY HUGHES, PRIME MINISTER OF AUSTRALIA. PLEASED TO MAKE YOUR ACQUAINTANCE.

ARTHUR

VERY GOOD. THE KING WISHES TO SEE JOSEPH IMMEDIATELY, BILLY, SO WE MUST GO. HE IS BEING CONSIDERED FOR A KNIGHTHOOD.

COOK

A KNIGHTHOOD?

ARTHUR

YES. ALL YOUR WORK REFORMING AND MANAGING THE NAVY HAS NOT GONE UNNOTICED BY THE KING, AND HE WISHES TO REWARD YOU BY KNIGHTING YOU SIR JOSEPH COOK.

COOK

MY WORD! IS THIS TRUE?

ARTHUR

IT IS MY FRIEND. MAY I BE THE FIRST TO SAY CONGRATULATIONS.

COOK

THIS IS SUCH AN HONOUR. WE HAVE JUST FINISHED HERE, SO I CAN COME RIGHT AWAY.

HUGHES

GO JOSEPH. I WILL TAKE CARE OF ANY OTHER BUSINESS. CONGRATULATIONS ON YOUR ACCOMPLISHMENT.

(EXIT HUGHES. ARTHUR AND COOK WALK TOGETHER TO THE OTHER SIDE OF THE STAGE.)

COOK

THIS IS AMAZING NEWS ARTHUR. I MUST TELL MARY AS SOON AS WE HAVE FINISHED.

ARTHUR

THERE IS NO NEED MY FRIEND. I HAVE ALREADY LET HER KNOW. SHE IS WAITING AT BUCKINGHAM PALACE WITH THE KING.

COOK

HOW WERE YOU ABLE TO DO ALL OF THIS ARTHUR?

ARTHUR

YOU KNOW ME JOSEPH I HAVE MY WAYS. IT WAS NO TROUBLE AT ALL. NO TROUBLE AT ALL. SHALL WE CONTINUE ON TO THE PALACE?

(EXIT ARTHUR AND COOK. ENTER KING GEORGE V AND MARY.)

KING GEORGE V

YOU MUST BE VERY PROUD OF YOUR HUSBAND MRS COOK, FOR ALL THE WORK HE HAS DONE FOR OUR COUNTRY.

MARY

YES, HE ALWAYS WORKED HARD WHETHER IT BE FOR HIS COUNTRY OR HIS FAMILY.

(ENTER ARTHUR AND COOK. COOK KNEELS BEFORE THE KING.)

KING GEORGE V

YOUR WIFE WAS JUST INFORMING ME ABOUT YOUR RELENTLESS PASSION FOR WORK MR COOK.

COOK

YES YOUR MAJESTY.

KING GEORGE V

YOU SHOULD BE PROUD. A MAN WHO IS WILLING TO RISK IT ALL FOR HIS COUNTRY AND HIS FAMILY IS WORTHY ENOUGH OF A KNIGHTHOOD, BUT YOU DESERVE THIS MORE THAN MOST. YOU HAVE DEMONSTRATED GREAT HONOUR, COURAGE AND RESOURCEFULNESS IN TIMES OF GREAT PERIL.

COOK

THANK YOU YOUR MAJESTY.

KING GEORGE V

HENCEFORTH, I DECLARE THAT FROM THIS DAY YOU SHALL BE KNOWN AS THE RIGHT AND HONOURABLE SIR JOSEPH COOK. ARISE, KNIGHT OF THE REALM.

(COOK STANDS)

I AM VERY IMPRESSED WITH YOUR WORK OVERSEAS SIR JOSEPH COOK. YOU KNOW HOW TO MANAGE A COUNTRY WELL.

COOK

THANK YOU. THIS IS A GREAT HONOUR FOR ME.

KING GEORGE V

YOUR SKILLS COULD PROVE MOST USEFUL TO THIS COUNTRY, IF YOU ACCEPT THE ROLE OF HIGH COMMISSIONER AFTER YOUR WORK IN AUSTRALIA IS FINISHED.

COOK

HIGH COMMISSIONER! BUT THAT WOULD MEAN I WOULD BE REPLACING...

(ENTER FISHER. EXIT KING GEORGE V.)

FISHER

HELLO COOK. I SEE YOU HAVE NOT CHANGED SINCE WE LAST MET. I SEE YOU HAVE BROUGHT A FRIEND WITH YOU. STILL UNABLE TO STAND ON YOUR OWN TWO FEET I SEE.

ARTHUR

HEY! YOU WILL NOT TALK TO MY FRIEND LIKE THAT.

FISHER

I DO NOT CARE IF YOUR FRIEND IS A KNIGHT OF THE REALM OR NOT, I WILL SPEAK TO HIM HOWEVER I PLEASE.

COOK

(LAUGHS)

YOU ARE VERY FUNNY FISHER. YOU HAVE ALWAYS BEEN A CLEVER MAN, YET YOU CAN NEVER SEE THE TRUTH. EVEN WHEN IT IS STARING YOU IN THE FACE YOU CANNOT SEE IT.

FISHER

YOU ARE MISTAKEN. I SEE THE TRUTH CLEARLY, YOU HAVE COME FOR MY JOB. BUT I MUST DISAPPOINT YOU. THIS WILL STILL BE MY JOB FOR AT LEAST ANOTHER COUPLE OF YEARS. THE TRUTH ESCAPES YOU JOE. IT ALWAYS HAS, AND IT ALWAYS WILL.

COOK

NO, NO, NO. YOU CANNOT SEE THE IRONY. CALL ME WEAK AND YET YOU HAVE SPENT THE LAST FOUR YEARS HERE IN ENGLAND HIDING AWAY BEHIND A DESK, WHILE BILLY AND I HAVE BEEN LEADING THE CHARGE BACK IN AUSTRALIA. YOU ABANDONED US THE MINUTE I ANNOUNCED THAT WAR HAD BROKEN OUT BECAUSE YOU WANTED TO GUARANTEE SAFETY FOR YOURSELF.

(COOK OFFERS FISHER A WHITE FEATHER)

FISHER

I DID WHAT I HAD TO IN ORDER TO SURVIVE THE WAR. YOU AND THAT TRAITOR BILLY WOULD KNOW NOTHING ABOUT IT.

COOK

BECAUSE WE ARE REAL MEN WHO CHOOSE TO LIVE IN THE REAL WORLD. WHEN WE HAVE PROBLEMS, WE CHOOSE TO CONFRONT THEM, AND I RESPECT BILLY FOR THIS.

(EXIT FISHER)

ARTHUR

WHAT AN UNPLEASANT MAN.

MARY

YOU HAVE NO IDEA ARTHUR.

(EXEUNT)

ACT III

SCENE 11

(A FEW DAYS LATER. MARY, COOK AND ARTHUR ARE SITTING BESIDES THE THAMES FISHING.)

COOK

SO HOW DID YOU END UP AS AN ENGINEER ARTHUR?

ARTHUR

IT WAS A MINING ACCIDENT. I WAS IN THE MIDDLE OF A MINOR COLLAPSE.

MARY

I AM SORRY ARTHUR.

ARTHUR

THERE IS NO NEED. I FELT VERY LUCKY THAT DAY NOT TO BE DEAD IN THE GROUND. MY RIGHT LEG HAS NEVER REALLY BEEN THE SAME. BUT WORKING IN THE MINES WAS MY LIFE, SO I DECIDED TO STUDY FOR MY MINING QUALIFICATIONS.

COOK

REALLY? I NEVER SAW YOU HAVING A DESK JOB ARTHUR. YOU ALWAYS SEEMED VERY CONTENT AT THE COALFACE.

ARTHUR

OH YES. I DECIDED TO START MY OWN COMPANY TO HELP INNOVATION IN THE MINING INDUSTRY.

COOK

YOU CONTINUE TO AMAZE ME MY FRIEND. YOU HAVE COME A LONG WAY SINCE WE WERE YOUNG.

ARTHUR

SAYS THE EX PRIME MINISTER OF AUSTRALIA.

COOK

I AM SERIOUS MY FRIEND. YOU HAVE BECOME A VERY SUCCESSFUL MAN
AND FOR THAT YOU SHOULD BE PROUD.

ARTHUR

AND SO SHOULD YOU JOSEPH. OVER TIME WE HAVE BECOME GREATER MEN
THAN EITHER OF US HAD IMAGINED. SPEAKING OF WHICH, WHAT IS THE
TIME?

MARY

IT IS NEARLY NOON.

ARTHUR

I HAD BEST BE OFF THEN. I SHALL SEE YOU BOTH AT DINNER
TONIGHT.

MARY

OF COURSE ARTHUR, WE WOULD NOT MISS THAT FOR THE WORLD.

ARTHUR

SPLENDID.

(EXIT ARTHUR)

COOK

I USED TO LOVE FISHING YOU KNOW. I REMEMBER MY FATHER USED TO
TAKE ME AND MY BROTHERS DOWN TO THE CANAL AT WEEKENDS. WE
WOULD FISH ALL DAY LONG AND REAP THE REWARDS OF A GOOD DAY OF
WORK.

MARY

IDEALS THAT HAVE STUCK WITH YOU THROUGH YOUR WHOLE LIFE.

COOK

I WOULD NOT KNOW ABOUT THAT. I SUPPOSE I HAVE ALWAYS WORKED
HARD BECAUSE MY FATHER TAUGHT ME THAT WORK IS THE GATEWAY TO A
BETTER LIFE. YET EVERY DAY I BEGIN TO THINK HE WAS WRONG.

MARY

BUT HE WAS RIGHT JOSEPH. YOU HAVE ACCOMPLISHED SO MUCH OVER
THE YEARS.

COOK

YET WAR AND TRAGEDY STILL EXIST. I CANNOT HELP BUT ASK MYSELF
WHETHER MY ACCOMPLISHMENTS MEAN ANYTHING.

MARY

THAT IS WHY WE MUST GO ON JOSEPH. TO KEEP WORKING, TO KEEP
LEARNING FROM OUR MISTAKES. YOU HAVE WORKED HARD EVER SINCE
YOU WERE YOUNG AND YOU SHOULD NOT BE ASHAMED OF THAT.

COOK

I AM NOT ASHAMED. I ONLY WISH I COULD HAVE STOPPED PEOPLE LIKE
FISHER AND LYNE FROM CONTROLLING AND MANIPULATING ME EVERY
STEP OF THE WAY.

MARY

YOU DO NOT NEED TO JUDGE YOURSELF BECAUSE OF THE ACTIONS OF OTHERS AROUND YOU. ESPECIALLY WHEN THESE PEOPLE NEVER WANTED THE BEST FOR YOU. JOSEPH COOK IS A MAN WHO HAS WORKED HARD ALL HIS LIFE AND YOUR REWARD IS YOUR KNIGHTHOOD. YOU ARE NO LONGER A PAWN, YOU ARE A MAN AND YOUR FATHER WOULD BE MORE THAN PROUD.

(COOK AND MARY EMBRACE EACH OTHER. MARY PLACES HER HEAD ON COOK'S SHOULDER.)

COOK

I LOVE YOU MARY.

MARY

I LOVE YOU TOO JOSEPH.

(EXEUNT)

155

North
Staffordshire
Press

Staffordshire
Chambers of
Commerce

SMALL PRESS
OF THE YEAR

The
British
Book
Awards
2019

Regional Finalist